The County Seats of the Noblemen and Gentlemen of Great Britain and Ireland. vol. 1, 2. (Vol. 3-5. A Series of Picturesque Views of Seats of the Noblemen ... of Great Britain and Ireland. With descriptive letterpress.).

Francis Orpen Morris

The County Seats of the Noblemen and Gentlemen of Great Britain and Ireland. vol. 1, 2. (Vol. 3-5. A Series of Picturesque Views of Seats of the Noblemen ... of Great Britain and Ireland. With descriptive letterpress.).

Morris, Francis Orpen
British Library, Historical Print Editions
British Library
1866-80
5 vol. ; 4°.
10360.k.20.

THE

County Seats

OF THE

Noblemen and Gentlemen

OF

GREAT BRITAIN AND IRELAND.

EDITED BY

THE REV. F. O. MORRIS, B.A.,

Rector of Nunburnholme, Yorkshire.

AUTHOR OF A "HISTORY OF BRITISH BIRDS," DEDICATED BY PERMISSION TO HER MAJESTY THE QUEEN.

"It is a reverend thing to see an ancient castle or building not in decay, or to see a fair timber tree sound and perfect; how much more to behold an ancient family which hath stood against the waves and weathers of time."—*Bacon.*

LONDON:
LONGMANS, GREEN, AND CO., PATERNOSTER ROW.

NOTICE.

The Editor returns his best thanks for obliging assistance towards this Work, to W. R. Tate, Esq., Grove Place, London; E. T. Burr, Esq., Cloudesley Square, London; James H. Lees, Esq., Lees, Lancashire; Sir C. H. Anderson, Bart., Lea, near Gainsborough; Mrs. Dent, Sudeley Castle, Gloucestershire; The Rev. Robert Brown, Sudeley; Sir J. Bernard Burke, The Castle, Dublin; Mrs. Robson, Wilton; The Right Hon. Lord Herries, Everingham Park, York; O. S. Round, Esq., Lincoln's Inn; The Rev. W. Bree, Allesley Rectory, near Coventry; Admiral Mitford, Hunmanby Hall; The Rev. C. Maber, Howsham; Mrs. Phillips, Picton Castle; Mrs. Burrows, Sunnyside; The Rev. M. G. Hubback, Eckington; Mrs. Admiral Mitford, Hunmanby Hall; Lady Sitwell, Reinshaw Hall; Miss Charlotte Hull; — Baker, Esq.; H. Onslow Piercy, Esq.

THE
County Seats

Of the

Noblemen and Gentlemen

Of

GREAT BRITAIN AND IRELAND

COUNTY SEATS

OF THE

NOBLEMEN AND GENTLEMEN

OF

GREAT BRITAIN AND IRELAND.

EDITED BY

THE REV. F. O. MORRIS, B.A.,

AUTHOR OF A "HISTORY OF BRITISH BIRDS," DEDICATED BY PERMISSION TO HER MAJESTY THE QUEEN.

VOL. I.

LONDON:

LONGMANS, GREEN, AND CO., PATERNOSTER ROW.

CONTENTS.

CONTENTS.

WINDSOR CASTLE.

THE COUNTY SEATS.

WINDSOR CASTLE,

THE ROYAL RESIDENCE.

THE history of Windsor Castle is the history of England and of England's Kings and Queens. To do it justice would require a far abler pen than mine, and far more space than is allowed by the narrow limits of a work like the present. The building is worthy of England, and of the long and illustrious line of monarchs who have sat upon our throne, and though there are many more striking and more picturesque situations to be found among those that abound in the broad lands of the island, there is perhaps none more thoroughly suitable for the Palace of the Ruling Sovereign of England, inasmuch as there is none more thoroughly English in its character and features.

Standing as it does on a gentle eminence in a part of the country which is neither flat nor mountainous, and surrounded as far as the eye can reach by beautiful Home scenery of a similar character, the winding Thames completes the beauty of the landscape, and at the same time carries to the ocean the story of the events which unite for ever its own name with those of Britain, thence to be borne by our ships of native oak to every corner of the globe—a world-wide history, the History of England.

Windsor Castle, originally a fortress of the Roman invaders, and probably of previous existence, was founded by WILLIAM the CONQUEROR, and has, as might be supposed, received numberless alterations and additions since. According to some historians, it was newly built by Henry I., where, in 1122, he celebrated his marriage with his second Queen, Adeliza of Louvain.

In the centre of the building, and raised on a mound, is the keep, or round tower, from which a full view of the surrounding country is obtained.

In 1170 a Parliament was held in the fortress under Henry II., in which *William the Lion*, King of Scotland, and his brother David attended as feudal barons of the realm.

Henry III. added greatly to the fortifications.

Edward I. held a grand tournament in the adjoining park.

Edward III. was born here, hence called *Edward of Windsor*. This monarch made great improvements in the Castle and town.

These vast works were superintended by the celebrated William of Wykeham, afterwards Bishop of Winchester, and the munificent founder of New College, Oxford, who was appointed keeper of the Manors of Old and New Windsor in 1359. On the Winchester Tower there is still to be seen a stone on which are cut the words "Hoc fecit Wykeham." The king on seeing the words "was exceedingly wroth against Wykeham, and but for his dexterity the affair would have gone seriously with the architect. Being summoned into the king's presence, the king demanded his explanation, when Wykeham told the king he read the inscription wrongly; it was not '*that Wykeham made the tower, but that the tower made Wykeham,*' whereat the king's wroth was appeased."

In this reign King John of France and King David of Scotland were both prisoners together in the Castle.

Henry VII. made various alterations in it.

Queen Elizabeth constructed the terrace walk on the north side.

During the civil wars in the reign of Charles I., Windsor Castle was garrisoned by the rebel troops. It was unsuccessfully attacked by Prince Rupert in the autumn of 1642; and in 1648 it became the prison of the unfortunate monarch.

Charles II. repaired and richly furnished it.

In the year 1824 the sum of £300,000 was voted by the nation for the general improvement of the Castle, and subsequent grants have raised the amount appropriated for the buildings alone to nearly £800,000.

It has in modern times been the favourite residence of King George III., King George IV., who greatly enriched it, William IV., and QUEEN VICTORIA, whom may GOD preserve.

The Chapel of St. George was given its present form by Edward IV., and was completed by King Henry VII. It is within it that the Knights of the Garter are installed, and the long lines of their banners that float from under its roof, are in themselves a history which connect it more or less nearly with almost the whole of the nobility and gentry of the country—a commingling of ranks, from the scions of Royalty down to the Commons of the land, which has had vast influence in making England the mighty and happy country that it is.

The state apartments are as follows:—

The Queen's Audience Chamber. Three sides of the room are hung with Gobelin tapestry, representing—Esther confided to the care of Hegai; the triumph of Mordecai; the crowning of Queen Esther by Ahasuerus. It contains also a portrait of the grandfather of King William III., by Honthorst; a portrait of the father of the King, by Honthorst; a whole-length portrait of Mary Queen of Scots, by Janet; a portrait of Frederick Henry, Prince of Orange, by Honthorst; and of William II., by Honthorst.

The Vandyke Room contains no fewer than twenty-two paintings by Vandyke, namely,—1. Henry, Comte de Bergh. 2. Charles I., Queen Henrietta, Prince Charles, and Prince James. 3. Mary, Duchess of Richmond. 4. Thomas Killigrew, and Thomas Carew. 5. Henrietta Maria, Queen of Charles I. 6. Lady Venetia Digby. 7. George Villiers, and Lord Francis Villiers. 8. Prince of Carignan. 9. Henrietta Maria. 10. Beatrix de Cusance, Princess de Cantecroy. 11. Five Children of Charles I.,—Prince Charles; James, Duke of York, and the Princesses Mary, Elizabeth, and Anne. 12. Charles I. 13. Henrietta Maria. 14. Lucy, Countess of Carlisle. 15. Sir Kenelm Digby. 16. Prince Charles, afterwards Charles II. 17. The Artist's own Portrait. 18. Henrietta Maria. 19. Three Children of Charles I., namely,—Prince Charles (Charles II.;) Princess Royal (Mary, Princess of Orange;) and Prince James, (James II.) 20. Mary, Countess of Dorset. 21. Charles I. on horseback. 22. A portrait of a person unknown.

Upon the crimson silk damask hangings are displayed the insignia of the Orders of the Garter, Bath, St. Patrick, and the Thistle.

The Queen's State Drawing Room is adorned with fourteen paintings, nine of them by Zuccarelli, namely,—1. The Meeting of Isaac and Rebecca. 2. The Finding of Moses, (painted expressly for George III., the artist being left to the choice of his subject.) 3 to 9. Seven large landscapes, one of which represents Jacob tending the flocks of Laban. 10. Portraits of Henry, Duke of Gloucester, when a child, the youngest son of Charles I. 11. George I., by Fountaine. 12. George II. 13. George III. 14. Frederick, Prince of Wales.

The rich silk hangings are ornamented with the arms of William IV. and Queen Adelaide.

The State Ante-Room contains beautiful specimens of carving of fruit, fowl, fish, and flowers, by Gibbons; and a portrait on stained glass of George III., in his coronation robes.

The Grand Staircase has several suits of armour of the sixteenth century, military trophies, a sculpture of an infant Hercules, antique study, etc.

The Waterloo Chamber, in which many of the state banquets are given, has a series of thirty-eight portraits, confined to those distinguished personages who were connected either in an immediate or accessory manner with the battle of Waterloo. The portraits were all painted by Sir Thomas Lawrence, except those otherwise mentioned. 1. Le Duc de Richelieu. 2. General Overoff. 3. Duke of Cambridge. 4. Right Hon. R. B. Jenkinson, second Earl of Liverpool, K.G. 5. William IV., (by Sir David Wilkie.) 6. George III., (by Sir William Beechy.) 7. George IV. 8. Viscount Castlereagh, K.G. 9. Duke of York, K.G. 10. Baron Von Humboldt. 11. Right Hon. George Canning. 12. Right Hon. Henry Bathurst, third Earl of Bathurst, K.G. 13. Count Munster. 14. Cardinal Ercole Gonsalvi. 15. Prince of Hardenburgh. 16. William III., King of Prussia. 17. Francis I., Emperor of Austria. 18. Alexander I., Emperor of Russia. 19. Count Nesselrode. 20. Pope Pius VII. 21. Count Capo d' Istrias. 22. Prince of Metternich-Winneberg.

23. Viscount Hill, G.C.B., (by H. W. Pickersgill, R.A.) 24. Charles X., King of France. 25. Prince of Schwartzenberg. 26. Archduke of Austria. 27. Lieutenant-General Sir Thomas Picton, G.C.B., (by Sir Martin Archer Shee, P.R.A.) 28. Duke of Angouleme. 29. William Frederick, Duke of Brunswick-Oels. 30. The King of the Belgians. 31. General Sir James Kempt, G.C.B., (by H. W. Pickersgill, R.A.) 32. Count Platoff. 33. Duke of Wellington, K.G. 34. Gelhard Von Blucher, Prince of Wahstadt. 35. Count Alten, G.C.B., and G.C.H., (by Reichmann.) 36. Marquis of Anglesea, K.G., (by Sir M. A. Shee, P.R.A.) 37. Lieutenant-General Count Czernitschoff. 38. William Frederick George Lewis, Prince of Orange.

The chimney-pieces, and some of the picture-frames, etc., are encircled with carvings by Gibbons of wreaths of fruit, flowers, etc.

The Presence Chamber is embellished with some magnificent specimens of Gobelin tapestry, illustrating the history of Jason and the Golden Fleece. It also contains the rare and costly Malachite vase presented to the Queen by the Emperor of Russia; and two exquisitely worked vases of granite, a present from the King of Prussia to King William IV.

St. George's Hall, two hundred feet in length, thirty-four feet wide, and thirty-two feet high, has whole-length portraits of the following sovereigns:—James I. and Charles I., by Vandyke; Charles II. and James II., by Sir Peter Lely; Mary, William III., Anne, and George I., by Sir Godfrey Kneller; George II., by Zeeman; George III., by Gainsborough; and George IV., by Sir Thomas Lawrence. Also on twenty-four shields, behind the throne or chair of state, are the arms of each sovereign of the Order of the Garter, from the time of its institution in the reign of Edward III. to King William IV. Also four knights in complete armour, one representing the founder of the order, and the other his son, Edward the Black Prince.

The Guard Chamber is nearly eighty feet in length, and thirty-one feet high. It contains the bust of Lord Nelson, by Sir Francis Chantrey, its pedestal being part of the mast of the *Victory* shot through by a cannon-ball. There are also busts of the great Duke of Marlborough, from Rysbach, and the Duke of Wellington, by Sir F. Chantrey, with their respective banners over them, by the annual presentation of which, on the anniversaries of the victories of Blenheim and Waterloo, the families of those two of England's greatest generals hold the estates of Blenheim and Strathsfieldsaye. Also two brass guns captured by Lord Hardinge in India, two taken by Lord Cornwallis at the storming of Seringapatam; and whole-length figures in armour of the Duke of Brunswick, 1530; Lord Howard, 1588; the Earl of Essex, 1596; Henry, Prince of Wales, 1612; Prince Rupert, 1635. There is also a collection of arms of various kinds tastefully arranged on the walls, and the famous shield by Benvenuto Cellini, said to have been presented by Francis I. of France to Henry VIII. on the "Field of the Cloth of Gold."

The Queen's Presence Chamber has its walls decorated with Gobelin tapestry, representing a continuation of the events in the life of Queen Esther; and other pictures, namely,—1. A full-length portrait of the Princess Elizabeth of Brunswick, (1649,) and her sister, by Mytens. 2. The Princess Dorothea, by the same master.

3. Henrietta (the wife of Philip, Duke of Orleans, brother of Louis XIV.,) and her two daughters, by Mignard.

The Gold Pantry contains a vast quantity of rare and costly articles, of which the following are but a few:—

The celebrated "Huma," representing a bird studded with precious stones, and captured from Tippoo Saib at the storming of Seringapatam, supposed to be of the value of upwards of £30,000.

The National Cup, richly embossed with the figures of St. George, St. Patrick, and St. Andrew; the Rose, the Shamrock, and the Thistle, formed of precious stones surmounted by imperial crowns.

"Amongst the numerous shields here deposited is the celebrated shield of Achilles, of exquisite design and workmanship. It is impossible to describe, with anything like accuracy, the beauties of the various salvers, vases, tankards, cups, epergnes, candelabra, etc.; they are all executed by the first artists, and the most refined tastes. We may, however, briefly refer to the celebrated candelabrum of St. George, which may be thus described:—The upper division represents the combat of St. George and the Dragon in full relief. The lower division has also in full relief four figures supporting shields, bearing the arms of England, Ireland, and Scotland, and the Prince of Wales's plume.

Many of the epergnes are embellished with sculptured subjects from the designs of Flaxman. There is also a very curious silver cup, made out of Spanish dollars taken at the surrender of Havannah in 1702, and presented to George IV., when Prince of Wales, on his twenty-first birthday, in 1783, by Sir J. Dyer. There are several bulb cups, some splendidly ornamented; others, of ivory, highly sculptured with allegorical devices from Flaxman's designs, richly mounted in gold, and adorned with rare brilliants and other precious stones."

The Private Apartments, which can only be viewed by an order obtained from the Lord Chamberlain, and then only when the Sovereign is not residing at Windsor, consist of

The Corridor, containing busts of Queen Victoria; Queen Anne; George I.; George II.; George III.; George IV.; William IV.; and Ferdinand, King Consort of Portugal. Prince Albert; Prince George of Cumberland; Prince George of Cambridge; and a son of the King of the Belgians. Princess Royal, and Princess Charlotte. Dukes of York, Kent, Cumberland, Cambridge, Gloucester, Edward of York, Wellington, Bedford, Devonshire, Gordon, and Villiers, Duke of Buckingham. Marquis of Granby, and Marquis of Anglesea. Earl of Harcourt, Earl Grey, and Francis, Earl of Moira. Countess of Charlemont. Viscount Castlereagh, and Viscount Lake. Lords Erskine, Ellenborough, Thurlow, and Granville, Baron Ligonier, and Lord Melbourne. Sir Robert Peel, Sir Thomas Hardy, Sir Geoffrey Wyatville, Sir Isaac Newton, and Sir Richard Keates. Archbishop Markham. Pope Pius. Cardinal Gonzalvi. Pitt, Fox, Pope, Shakespeare, Sheridan, Handel, Sebastian Le Prestre, Marshal, Dr. Johnson, Garrick, Boyle, Clark, Locke, Bacon, Platoff, Blucher, etc.

The White Drawing Room. The Green Drawing Room. The Crimson Drawing Room. The Queen's Private Boudoir. The Private Dining Room. The Grand Reception

Room. The Rubens Room. The Picture Gallery. The Purple Throne Room. The Library. St. George's Hall. The Prince Consort's Painting Room. The Private Chapel.

The buildings occupy about twelve acres of ground.

The Castle is open to visitors on Mondays, Tuesdays, Thursdays, and Fridays.

––––––––

The Royal Family of England descends from Guelph, younger brother of Odoacer, conqueror and first barbarian King of Italy, who died in the year 489.

HAREWOOD HOUSE.

HAREWOOD HOUSE,

NEAR WETHERBY, YORKSHIRE.—EARL OF HAREWOOD.

———

HAREWOOD HOUSE, the magnificent residence of the Earl of Harewood, is beautifully situated in a noble and gracefully undulated Park of upwards of two thousand acres, and looks down over a garden, which in summer is a very blaze of flowers of every hue, upon a fine lake in front. Behind it, a few hundred yards off, on the other side of the hill on which it stands, are the ruins of Harewood Castle, overlooking the valley of the Wharfe, from which in a westerly direction a lovely view of Wharfedale is bounded by the Craven mountains, nearly twenty miles away; while towards the east the great vale of York stretches out, with York Minster rising up from it at about the like distance.

In the year 1080 William the Conqueror gave Harewood, with other large estates in Yorkshire, to

ROBERT DE ROMELLI, said by Gabriel de Moulin to have been of an ancient and eminent family in Normandy. He had an only daughter,

CECILY DE ROMELLI, married to William de Meschines, Earl of Chester, who thus became, in 1120, Lord of Harewood. They founded a Priory at Embsay, in Craven, which was afterwards removed by their daughter Avicia to Bolton Abbey. They had issue—

1. Rafe, died without children.
2. Matthew, died issueless.
3. Alice, married to Fitz-Duncan, son of the Earl of Murray, nephew to Malcolm, King of Scotland.
4. Avicia, married to William de Courcy, of Stoke Courcy, in the county of Somerset, Steward of the Household to King Henry I.

The two daughters being co-heiresses of vast estates and wealth, retained their surnames after marriage, and the latter,

AVICIA (DE COURCY) DE ROMELLI, had by her husband a son, drowned in leaping over the Strid, a narrow chasm in the rocks between which the river Wharfe flows, above Bolton Abbey:

> "He sprang in glee, for what cared he
>   That the river was strong and the rocks were steep;
> But the greyhound in the leash hung back,
>   And checked him in his leap;
> And never more was young Romilly seen
>   Till he rose a lifeless corse."

Wordsworth and Rogers have both recorded this event. There are, however, doubts about the truth of the legend, and Dr. Whitaker imagines it may refer to one of the sons of the first foundress of the Abbey of Embsay, both of whom died young; and it is supposed by many that the story was an invention of the monks, in order to remove from the cold and cheerless heights of Embsay to the lovely seclusion of the valley where Bolton Abbey now stands, the extreme beauty of which is exceeded by no scenery in England.

The manor of Harewood then descended, in 1180, to the eldest son of William and Avicia, (de Courcy,)

DE ROMELLI, whose daughter carried it by marriage into the family of

FITZGERALD, in 1195, which was followed by that of

DE BREANT, 1225.

DE REDVERS, 1240.

DE FORTIBUS, 1270.

EARL OF LANCASTER, 1274. (Edward Crouchback, second son of King Henry III.)

LORD LISLE, 1300.

DE ALDEBURGH, 1365. He had two daughters, co-heiresses of the Harewood estates, namely,

ELIZABETH, married Sir R. Redman, or Redmayne,

SYBILL, married Sir William Ryther.

GASCOIGNE, in 1545, Marmaduke Gascoigne marrying the daughter and heiress of Henry Redmayne, Esq.

WENTWORTH, ancestor of Lord Strafford, 1580, by marriage with Margaret, daughter and heiress of William Gascoigne.

SIR JOHN CUTLER, 1693, (by purchase.)

EARL OF RADNOR, 1693, (by marriage with Elizabeth, daughter and heiress of Sir John Cutler.)

BOULTER, 1696, (by will of Sir John Cutler, in failure of a direct heir.)

LASCELLES, 1739, (by purchase,) ancestor of the Earls of Harewood.

Among the paintings at Harewood House are two views of Plompton Rocks by Turner; Richmond Castle, Knaresborough Castle, Aisgarth Force, and Harewood Castle, by Dahl; Henry, second Earl of Harewood, by Jackson; Mr. Pitt, Henrietta, wife of the second Earl, Lady Worsley, Mrs. Hale and five children, and Edward, Earl of Harewood, his wife, and child, by Sir Joshua Reynolds; Lady Frances Hope, Lady Cavendish, Mr. Arthur Lascelles, and Mr. Edwin Lascelles, in a group; Edward, first Lord Harewood, and Jane, Countess of Harrington; Lady Mary Yorke, daughter of the first Earl, and Edwin, Viscount Lascelles, both by Hopper; Louisa, Dowager Countess, wife of the third Earl, by Richmond, presented by the tenants of the estate; Henry, third Earl, on horseback, by Grant, R.A., presented by the members of the Bramham Moor Hunt; and Henry, second Earl of Harewood, a full-length portrait by Sir Thomas Lawrence, presented to the Countess of Harewood by a numerous body of the freeholders of the county of York.

The family of Lascelles, Earls of Harewood, derives from John de Lascelles, of Hinderskelfe, (now called Castle Howard,) in the Wapentake of Bulmer, in the North Riding of the county of York, living in 1315.

WILTON HOUSE.

WILTON HOUSE,

WILTON, WILTSHIRE.—EARL OF PEMBROKE AND MONTGOMERY.

WILTON HOUSE is an imposing structure, and the grounds immediately adjoin the town of Wilton, which is pleasantly situated on the junction of the rivers Nadder and Wiley, from the latter of which it derives its name. It was rebuilt, as to its present front, by Inigo Jones, a part of the previous mansion having been destroyed by fire in 1648.

In the year 773 an abbey was founded here by Weolkstan, Earl of Ellandum.

In 830 it was completed, when Egbert, King of England, converted it into a priory for thirteen nuns, and his sister Aburga was made prioress.

In the reign of Alfred the Great the priory was demolished by the Danes, but on their being expelled from the country he founded in its stead a monastery on the site where his palace had stood, and added a lady abbess and twelve nuns to its original foundation.

In the reign of Edgar, a lady named Walfrith being the abbess, it was again destroyed by Swein, in revenge for a massacre of the Danes.

It was afterwards restored, but in Ethelred's reign the Danes again invaded the country, and he was succeeded on the throne by a Danish monarch, followed by three others.

On the restoration of the Saxon kings the monastery was rebuilt by Edith, wife of Edward the Confessor. It was now constructed of stone, having previously been of wood.

In the year 1066 William the Conqueror obtained possession of the throne, and, as recorded in Domesday Book, doubled the value of the house, the abbess at that time being Christiana, sister of Edgar Atheling, and here she educated Matilda, her niece, who afterwards became wife of Henry Beauclerc.

During the civil wars that followed, Wilton met with its share of disaster.

In the year 1143 King Stephen arrived here with his brother, the Bishop of Winchester, and a large force, and began to convert the monastery into a place of military defence, but he was attacked in it by the Earl of Gloucester, and fled, when it again was sacked. It was, however, afterwards restored.

In the reign of Edward the First, Juliana Gifford being the abbess, a knight named Osborn Gifford carried off two of the nuns, with, as is hinted, their own assent.

In the reign of Henry the Eighth the monastery shared in the general dissolution of those institutions, the abbess being Cecilia Bodenham, and was shortly afterwards levelled with the ground. It was then granted by that monarch to Sir William Herbert, who was ancestor of the present Earl, and was made Earl of Pembroke by King Edward the Sixth, about the year 1560.

The principal paintings at Wilton House are the following:—The celebrated picture by Vandyke, seventeen feet in length by eleven feet in height, containing ten whole-length figures.—Philip, Earl of Pembroke, and his wife; their five sons—Charles Lord Herbert, Philip, William, James, and John; their daughter Anna Sophia, and her husband, Robert, Earl of Caernarvon; Lady Mary, daughter of the Duke of Buckingham, wife of Charles Lord Herbert, and above, in the clouds, two sons and a daughter who died young. King Charles the First and his Queen Henrietta; William Earl of Pembroke; the first wife of Philip, second Earl of that name; three children of Charles the First; the Duchess of Richmond and Mrs. Gibson; the Duke of Richmond and Lennox; the Countess of Castlehaven; Philip, the second Earl of that name; Sir William Herbert, the founder of the family; Sir Charles Hotham; the Duke of Montagu; Lady Rockingham; Frederick, Prince of Wales; Anne, Princess Royal; the Princess Amelia; the Princess Elizabeth; Sir Andrew Fountaine; Barbara, second wife of Thomas, Earl of Pembroke; an Architectural Design; another of the like kind; Dogs; Flemish Nobleman; the Woman taken in Adultery; Sea Victory; Virgin and Infant; Andromache fainting at the death of Hector; the discovery of Achilles; Fruit; Ark of Noah.

Thomas, eighth Earl of Pembroke, added to the collection, and removed to their present place the cabinets of Guistiniani and Valetta, and of Cardinal Mazarin and Cardinal Richelieu.

The armoury in the hall contains trophies and memorials of the battle of St. Quentin, in 1557, in which the Earl of Pembroke commanded the English forces. Among the curiosities are some fine specimens of horns and bones of the moose deer. The cedars in the grounds near the house are said to be the finest in England. There is also a magnificent specimen of the ilex, and a yew tree of remarkable extent opposite to the Park.

The House is shown to the public on stated days.

The Parish Church was rebuilt by the late Right Honourable Sidney Herbert, afterwards Lord Herbert of Lea, brother of the then Earl of Pembroke, at a cost of upwards of £60,000.

This family of Herbert is derived from Sir Richard Herbert, Knight, of Ewyas, a son of William, first Earl of Pembroke, who had been advanced to that dignity May 27th., 1472. The senior line descended from Sir William Herbert ap Thomas, living in the reign of Henry the Fifth, and who resided at Ragland Castle, in Monmouthshire, is represented by the family of Herbert of Muccruss Abbey, near Killarney, in the county of Kerry.

CASTLE HOWARD.

CASTLE HOWARD,

CASTLE HOWARD was anciently called Hinderskelfe, the word meaning Hundred-hill, or the place where the Hundreds meet, the Wapentakes, namely, of Bulmer and Ryedale.

It is finely situated in a well-wooded district, on a gentle eminence, in the centre of a tract of similar character, and looks down on one side on an extensive and ornamental lake.

Its history is as follows:—

In the year 1070 Malcolm, King of Scotland, ravaged the place.

The old castle of Hinderskelfe was built in the reign of Edward III., by the then Baron of Greystock.

RALF, Lord Greystock, left an only daughter,

ELIZABETH, who married Thomas, Lord Dacre of Gilsland, in which family it was continued till the marriage of

ELIZABETH, sister and coheir of George, Lord Dacre, with

LORD WILLIAM HOWARD, third son of Thomas, Duke of Norfolk, in consequence of which Hinderskelfe passed into the noble family of the Howards, in which it has since continued.

The ancient castle of Hinderskelfe being accidentally burnt down, the present edifice was raised on its site about the year 1702, by Charles, third Earl of Carlisle, then Earl Marshal of England, and the name of castle retained, though the building has no castellated features. Sir John Vanbrugh was the architect. It is always open to the public in the most liberal manner.

The museum contains a variety of valuable mosaics, marbles, etc.

The principal paintings at Castle Howard are upwards of seventy in number, containing, among others, specimens by Angeletti, three; Gia Bassano; Giovanni Bellini; John Bellini; Berghem; Boll; Breughel, three; Paul Brill; Burgonioni; Canaletti, three; Agostino Caracci; Annibal Caracci, four—one of these "The Three Marys," of the estimated value of which so many stories are told: one of them that the Court of Spain offered to cover its surface with Louis d' ors, which would amount to £8,000, and that an English offer exceeded that sum; Ludovico Caracci; Cooper; Correggio; Dahl; Domenichino; Domenico Fetë; Copley Fielding; Gainsborough, two; Orazio Gentileschi; Greffier; Guercino; Holbein, three; Hopner, four; Huysman; Cornelius Jansens, four; Jennet, or Holbein (?); Lance; Filippo Laura, two; Sir

Thomas Lawrence, two; Sir Peter Lely, ten; Cavalieri Liberi; Lilienbergh; Mabeuse; Carlo Maratti; Marlow; Mignard; Sir Anthony Moore; P. Panini; Juan de Paresa; Nicholas Poussin; Primatiecio; Rembrandt, three; Sir Joshua Reynolds, seven; Mario Ricci; Sebastian Ricci; Julio Romano; Salvator Rosa, four; Rottenhamer; Rubens, three; Saracino; Teniers the elder; Tintoretto, three; Titian, five; Rosa di Tivoli; Pierini del Vago; Vandevelde; Vandyke, five; Vangoyen; Paul Vansomer; Velasquez, three; Paul Veronese; Simon de Vos; Wouvermans, two; Zuccarelli; Zucchero, two. There are also others by Aikman, three; Sir George Beaumont; Dobson; Ellerby; Old Frank, three; Gale; Howard; Hudson; Jackson, eleven; Nicholson; Northcote; Proctor; Ross; Snow; Stone; Stubbs; Westall; Wheatley; Williams; Wissing; Wootton; and one of the Venetian School.

There are besides a large number of other paintings, upwards of sixty, more or less valuable, of which the artists' names are not satisfactorily known; and many valuable and beautiful statues, busts, and bronzes, besides paintings on the walls and ceilings.

The family of Howard descends from William Howard, an eminent lawyer, who was made Chief Justice of the Court of Common Pleas, and acted in that capacity from 1297 to 1308.

12 FE66

HOWSHAM HALL,

NEAR MALTON, YORKSHIRE.

HOWSHAM HALL, built, according to tradition, of stone brought from the neighbouring abbey of Kirkham, is very pleasantly situated on the south bank of the River Derwent, in a beautiful part of the valley about eight miles from Malton, and twelve from York. The winding river, with its hill-side woods, combine in giving a charming character to the local scenery, as any one will say who takes the private path that leads from the old grey mansion to the high grounds above Westowe, which afford an extensive and majestic view over a richly-wooded country, including the great plain of York, up to the West-Riding hills beyond Ripon, the district of Crayke, Castle Howard, and the North Yorkshire Moors, and on the other side part of the Wolds, Malton, and the country on to Scarborough.

This seat formerly belonged to the great Yorkshire family of Wentworth, and passed by marriage to the Cholmleys of Whitby Abbey.

The style of the architecture of the house appears to belong to the latter part of the reign of James II., but the building is stated to have been erected about the time of Queen Elizabeth.

Like most other old mansions, Howsham has its legend, being said to have been laid under a malison by St. Hilda, which story probably had its origin in the remarkable words of Sir Henry Spelman on the history of sacrilege, which were written to shew that the possession of church property entails, if one may say so, a failure of male heirs; and singular as the coincidence may appear in a vast number of instances, it is no less true as a matter of fact and melancholy history in many.

The whole of the building is surmounted by a curious ornamented parapet; over the front is a shield containing the four quarterings of the Cholmleys.

The family of Cholmley, now extinct in the male line of this branch, is descended from the ancient family of Cholmondeley, of Cholmondeley, in Cheshire, and the contraction of the name is stated to have taken place about the time of Henry VII. or Henry VIII. One of its members, Sir Hugh Cholmley, in the time of the civil war, bravely defended the Castle of Scarborough for more than twelve months against the Parliamentarian Army, and, during the whole time of the siege his lady remained with him in the castle, and attended the sick and wounded. At length, having surrendered on honourable terms, in 1645, Sir Hugh and his family went into exile; his estates were sequestered, and his seat at Whitby converted into a garrison, and plundered of everything valuable by the Parliamentarian troops. He continued in exile till 1649, when his brother, Sir Henry Cholmley, found means to appease the Parliament, and he was permitted to return to England. About the middle of the last century the family left their ancient seat at Whitby, which is situated on a hill on the west side of the town, between the church and the ruins of the Abbey, only a small part of which remains, and made Howsham their chief country residence. Nathaniel Cholmley, Esq., of Howsham, betook himself early to the profession of arms, and had his horse killed under him at the battle of Dettingen; but on the death of his father he retired to his paternal estate, and represented successively the towns of Aldborough and Boroughbridge in Parliament.

He was succeeded by the late Colonel George Cholmley, the last of his race, of whose uniform kindness and hospitality the author of the present work would be very forgetful, if he did not pay a willing tribute of grateful recollection to his memory.

A very handsome church for the hamlet of Howsham, which possessed none before, has been erected within the last few years at the sole cost of Mrs. Cholmley, his widow.

There are a number of fine and valuable portraits and other paintings at Howsham, among which are the following:—Sir William and Lady Anne Twisden, by Gerard. James Butler, Duke of Ormond, godfather of Lady Elizabeth Wentworth, by Lely. Sir Richard Cholmley the Black Knight, by Zuccero. Sir Hugh Cholmley, Governor of Scarborough Castle, by Lely. Sir Hugh Cholmley, of Whitby, fourth Baronet, Governor of Tangiers, by Lely. Hugh Cholmley, of Whitby and Howsham, by Jervais. Catherine, wife of Hugh Cholmley, Esq., only daughter of Sir John Wentworth, by Jervais. Nathaniel Cholmley, of Whitby, by Riley. Henrietta Catherine, daughter of Stephen Croft, Esq., second wife of Nathaniel Cholmley. Colonel George Cholmley, (the late.) Mrs. Hannah Cholmley, daughter of John Robinson Foulis, Esq., of Bucton Hall and Heslerton Hall, Yorkshire. George Cholmley, Esq., (late Grimes.) Mary, wife of Nathaniel Cholmley, Esq., and her three children, by Sir John Medina. Charles I. and child, by Vandyke. Henrietta, wife of Charles I., and child. William III. Mary II. James II. in buff armour, by Nicholas de Largilliere. Sir Henry Spielman. James Stuart, Duke of Richmond, and the dog that saved his life, by Vandyke. Virgin and Infant, by Corregio. Charles I. on horseback, by Vandyke.

There is besides a most curious and valuable series of eight ancient Spanish pictures, supposed to have come into possession of Sir Hugh Cholmley, of Tangiers, from a captured Dutch vessel, and originally mounted on cotton. They were brought from Whitby to Howsham. 1. Spanish Soldiers entering Tabasco, led by Geronimo de Aquila. 2. Cortez' arrival at Vera Cruz. 3. Cortez' reception at Xoloc by Montezuma. 4. Montezuma killed by the Indians, who also set fire to the houses of the Spaniards. 5. Cortez leaves Mexico pursued by the Indians. 6. The Capture of the Mexican Royal Standard. 7. The last combat in Mexico by Cortez and his soldiers. 8. Guatemozin, last King of Mexico—people trying to escape in canoes—taken by the Spaniards, which ended the siege.

The family of Cholmley deduces from Richard le Belward, whose younger grandson Robert le Belward, having had the lordship of Cholmundeleih, otherwise written Cholmondeley and Calmundelei, given him by his father, assumed that name in lieu of his own.

SUDELEY CASTLE.

SUDELEY CASTLE,

NEAR WINCHCOMBE, GLOUCESTERSHIRE.

"THY sun is set, thy battlements are fallen,
And sunk to ruin thy baronial hall,
Once far-famed Sudeley! Waves the cross no more
On thy reft towers; nor grins the leopard rude *
His feudal fierceness on thy tumbling roof."

SIR EGERTON BRYDGES.

"IN old times," says Camden, "certain noblemen here dwelt, and of it had their addition,

DE SUDELEY, descended of a right ancient English race, to wit, from Goda, King Ethelred's daughter, whose son,

RALF DE MEDERETINUS, Earl of Hereford, begat HAROLD, LORD OF SUDELEY, whose progeny flourished here for a long time."

"There had been a manor place at Sudeley," observes Leland, in his "Itinerary," "before the building of the castle, and the platte is yet seen in Sudeley Parke, where it stode."

WALTER DE MAUNT, Lord of Sudeley, married Goda, sister of King Edward the Confessor, and had,

HAROLD, surnamed *de Sutlei*, from the name of the place, who possessed it at the time of the Conquest in 1066. He was succeeded by

JOHN, followed by

RAPHE, who had two sons,

    1. Otvel.

    2. Raphe, the latter of whom,

RAPHE, succeeded, and next after him,

BARTHOLOMEW (Sir) de Sudle, Sheriff of Herefordshire, and Governor of Hereford Castle, and a Justice of Assize. He married Joan, daughter of William de Beauchamp, of Elmley, and sister of William, first Earl of Warwick of that name, and left issue

SIR JOHN de Sudeley, who was father of

BARTHOLOMEW, whose son

JOHN, had issue

    1. John.

    2. Joane, married Sir William Boteler, of Wemme, and had a son, THOMAS, who inherited the lordship.

---

* A leopard's head on a cross diamond was the coat of arms of the house of Chandos.

3. Margerie, married Sir Robert Massy, Knight.

The son,

JOHN, died without children, and was succeeded by the above-named

THOMAS BOTELER, (Sir) who was followed by his son

SIR RAPHE BOTELER, created Baron of Sudeley, and some time Governor of Calais. This nobleman built the castle of Sudeley, from the spoils, it is said, he had acquired in the wars with France. It was a splendid structure, and is described by Fuller as "of subjects' castles the most handsome habitation, and of subjects' habitations the strongest castle."

"At this splendid retirement it was that in the decline of life, and removed from courts and camps, the founder probably hoped tranquilly to pass the remainder of his days. But deceitful, often, is the smile of fortune, and liable to disappointment are human expectations. So fluctuating was the state of public affairs in his time, that the person and property of the subject were alike unsafe; and the favourite of one reign was generally obnoxious to the succeeding. On the fall of his unhappy royal master, he made an effort to have his attendance in parliament excused, on account of the infirmities of age; and his wishes were so far complied with, that he obtained letters patent from Edward IV., exempting him from that service during life. Yet this appearance of indulgence was not long continued; for, being suspected by the Yorkists of a strong attachment to the Lancastrian interest, he was apprehended at his castle, and conveyed prisoner to London, when, in order to avert worse consequences, he found himself compelled to sell both the manor of Sudeley and his princely mansion to the king."

Soon afterwards Sudeley Castle was granted to Richard, Duke of Gloucester, who exchanged it with the crown for Richmond Castle, in Yorkshire.

In the first year of the reign of Henry VII. it was bestowed on Jasper, Duke of Bedford, (younger son of Owen Tudor and his wife Catharine, widow of King Henry V. of England,) or, rather, was held by him for the owner; for, according to Leland, he "kept householde here," but it is not noticed among the estates of which he died seized. In the time of King Henry VIII., Leland wrote that "now it goeth to ruinne, more pittye."

In the reign of Edward VI. it was granted with the manor to Sir Thomas Seymour, uncle of the king, and brother of the Protector Somerset, who was then made

BARON SEYMOUR OF SUDELEY, and appointed Lord High Admiral. It was splendidly restored by him. He shortly afterwards married, in 1547, as her fourth husband, the DOWAGER QUEEN CATHERINE (PARR,) widow of KING HENRY THE EIGHTH, she having been deeply attached, and nearly contracted to him, before her almost compulsory marriage to the king.

While at Sudeley the Queen had under her charge the innocent and memorable LADY JANE GREY, whose untimely and sad fate need not be here recorded.

On the 13th. of June, 1548, the queen arrived at Sudeley for her confinement, and died on the 5th. of September, a week after the birth of a daughter named Mary. She was buried at Sudeley.

There is a curious MSS., discovered in the Herald's Office, entitled "A Boke of Buryalls of true noble persons." It furnishes at full length an account of the ceremonies performed at the funeral of the queen; to wit,

"A Breviate of th' entierment
of the lady Katheryn Parre
Quene Dowager late Wiefe
to Kinge Henry th' eight
and after wiefe to Sr Thomas lord
Seymer of Sudeley and highe
Admirall of Englond."

The following is the inscription over the tomb:—

K. P.

Here lyethe Quene
Kateryn Wife to Kyng
Henry the VIII. and
Last the Wife of Thomas
Lord of Sudeley, highe
Admyrall of Englond,
And vncle to Kyng
Edward the VI.
dyed
5 September
MCCCCC
xlviii.

Among the documents printed in the Burghley Papers is the following statement of Lady Elizabeth Tyrwhitt, which seems to be the deposition of one of the ladies in waiting made before the Privy Council when the bill of attainder was preparing against Seymour,

"A too dayes afor the deth of the Quen, at my cumyng to har in the mornyng, she askyd me where I had been so long, and sayed unto me, she dyd fere such things in harself that she was suer she cold not lyve: whereunto I answaryd, as I thowght that I sawe no lyklyhod of deth in har. She then hareyng my lord admyrall by the hand, and dyvers other standyng by, spake thes wardys, partly as I took hyt, idylly, 'My lady Tyrwhitt, I am not wel handelyd, for thos that be abowt me caryth not for me, but standyth lawghyng at my gref; and the moor good I wyl to them, the les good they wyl to me;' whereunto my lord admyrall answered, 'why swet-hart I would you no hurt,' and she saed to hym agayn aloud, 'no my lord, I thinke so,' and imedyetly she sayed to hym in his ere, 'but my lord, you have given me many shrowd tauntes.' Thos wordys I parsavwyd she spake with good memory, and very sharply and ernestly, for har mynd was for unquyetted. My lord admyrall parsevyng that I hard hyt, callyd me asyd, and askyd me what she sayd, and I declaryd hyt plainly to hym. Then he consowltyd with me that he wold lie down on the bed by har, to loke if he could pacyfy har unquyetnes wit gentyl camynycacyon; whereunto I agred. And by that time he had spoken thre or four wordes to har, she answered hym very rowndly and shortly, sayeing 'My lorde, I wolde have given a thousand markes to have had my full talk wyth Hewke the fyrst daye I was delyveryd, but I doorst not for displesyng of you:' and I heryng of that my hart wold sarve me to her no mor. Sych lyke comunycasyon she had with hym the space of an oar, wych they did hear that sat by har bed syde."

"Elizabeth Tyrwhitt."

Shortly after the death of the queen, Seymour paid court to the Princess Elizabeth, but his enemies were on the alert, and fomented the disagreement between him and his brother the Protector, when he was speedily committed to the Tower, condemned without a trial, and beheaded on Tower Hill, March 20th., 1549.

At his death Sudeley again reverted to the crown. It was then bestowed on the Marquis of Northampton, but he was shortly afterwards attainted for espousing the cause of Lady Jane Grey, and of course deprived of his estates.

It was next granted by Queen Mary to Sir John Brydges, who was one of the foremost in her train on her entrance into London, August 3rd., 1553, and attended her to the Tower, which she then committed to his custody for his services, and he was shortly afterwards raised to the peerage by the title of Baron Chandos of Sudeley. He fought at the "battle of the Spurs." He died on the 4th. of March, 1557, and was buried at Sudeley, and succeeded by his eldest son,

Edmund Brydges, K.G., who, like his father, engaged in military pursuits, and was knighted on the field by the Duke of Somerset, for his bravery in the battle of Musselberg. He married Lady Dorothy, daughter of Edward Lord Bray, the foundress of almshouses still standing at Winchcombe for twelve poor persons. His son and heir,

Giles, third Lord Chandos, lived a quiet country life, and had the honour of entertaining Queen Elizabeth at Sudeley, in one of her "Progresses," as recorded by Nichols. On this occasion he presented Her Majesty, it being, it appears, her custom to expect some such present from her hosts, with a splendid piece of jewelry attached to a gold chain, and consisting of a falcon or pheasant, the body crystal, the head, tail, legs, and breast of gold, fully garnished with sparks of rubies and emeralds.

He married Lady Frances, daughter of Edward, Earl of Lincoln, foundress of the Grammar School of Winchcombe, for fourteen scholars, natives of the place. He died in 1593, and was followed in the barony by his brother.

William Brydges, fourth Lord Chandos of Sudeley, married Mary, sister of Sir Owen Hopton, and was succeeded by his son,

Grey Bridges, fifth Lord. "This Lord," says Collins, "was a noble housekeeper, and by a winning behaviour contracted so great an interest in Gloucestershire, and had such numerous attendants when he came to court, that he was commonly called 'The King of Coteswold.' For, having an ample fortune, he expended it in the most generous manner; his Castle of Sudeley being kept open three days every week for the gentry, and the poor were as constantly fed with the remnants of his hospitable entertainments. In short, his ability and disposition were so exactly proportioned to each other, that it was difficult to determine which had the greatest share in his numberless acts of beneficence."

He married Anne, eldest daughter of Ferdinand, Earl of Derby, and died in Italy in 1621, but was interred at Sudeley with his ancestors, leaving a son, George, his heir, only then a year old.

This nobleman,

GEORGE, sixth LORD CHANDOS, was a distinguished cavalier, and raised a regiment of cavalry for the king, leaving his own castle guarded by Captain Brydges, which was attacked on January 1st., 1642, by Massie, Governor of Gloucester, with 300 Infantry and two pieces of Artillery. The castle was surrendered to him on certain conditions, which, though sworn to, were immediately basely broken on the part of the "Parliament Army raised for the defence of religion," who profaned the church, and utterly wasted the goods of the poor inhabitants of that place. In the following year Lord Chandos distinguished himself at the battle of Newbury, and had three horses killed under him; he mounted a fourth, and aided much in breaking the cavalry of the Parliament. It was feared he was running into too great danger, but Charles exclaimed, "Let Chandos, alone, his errors are safe." The king for his valour and services that day, desired to make him Earl of Newbury, but he modestly declined the offer "till it might please God to restore His Majesty to the peaceable enjoyment of his own." He recovered his castle the same year and intrusted the command to Sir William Morton, formerly a lawyer, but then fighting as an officer for the king. Shortly afterwards King Charles visited Sudeley Castle, and remained there during the siege of Gloucester. It was afterwards again besieged by Sir William Waller and Massie, and again capitulated, a shot having taken off the head of the captain of artillery, the place being but ill provided for a siege. The castle was almost irreparably destroyed in this and the former siege, and gave occasion for the verses placed at the head of this chapter. Lord Chandos died February 6th., 1654, (see BURKE's "Extinct and Dormant Peerages,") and was interred at Sudeley, and, having no son, bequeathed the greater part of his estates to Jane, his second wife, daughter of John Savage, Earl Rivers, and on her remarrying with George Pitt, Esq., of Strathfieldsaye, in Hampshire, ancestor of the Lords Rivers, the estate and manor of Sudeley passed into that family. In 1810 the then Lord Rivers sold the castle and a small part of the estate to the Duke of Buckingham.

Among the many valuable and interesting antiquities and works of art at Sudeley, are a portrait of King Henry VIII. and his children, by Sir Antonio More; The marriage of Henry VII. and Elizabeth of York, by Mabeuse; Charles I., by Vandyke; a portrait of Queen Elizabeth, by Zucchero; also two most valuable carvings of King Henry VIII., in bone, stone, and boxwood, by Holbein; a pietra dura table weighing nearly a ton, formed of the rarest and most valuable marbles, elaborately worked in intricate devices, and enriched with turquoise, lapis lazuli, etc., the stem gracefully carved and gilt, displaying the ducal arms of Tuscany. It formerly adorned the palace at Florence of Lorenzo de Medicis. Last, and chief, the autograph letter of Queen Katherine Parr to the admiral, in which she accepts him as her husband, and several personal relics of the Queen. A lock of her hair, found when the tomb was re-opened a second time, in July, 1807, (it having been previously opened in May, 1784, and October 14th., 1786,) was lent to Miss Agnes Strickland for the use of her work, by Mrs. Constable Maxwell, of Everingham Park. "It was of the most exquisite quality and colour, exactly resembling threads of burnished gold in its hue. It was very fine, and with an inclination to curl naturally."

The chapel, in the early perpendicular style, built in the latter part of the reign of Henry VI., was desecrated and defaced by Cromwell and his lawless troops. It remained roofless and ivy-clad for two centuries, but in 1858 its restoration was commenced, and it has been one of Mr. G. G. Scott's most happy efforts. A canopied tomb, with a recumbent figure of Queen Katherine Parr in white marble, and an alabaster sarcophagus, have been erected, and the remains of our first Queen of the restored faith have again found a fitting resting-place.

The lover of church restoration will be well repaid by a visit to her shrine: there is not a more perfect gem in this country. A choral service is now performed on each succeeding Lord's Day. A brass tablet near the door tells its story:—

"To the glory of God and to the memory of John Dent and William Dent, of Worcester and Sudeley Castle, this chapel, destroyed in the civil wars of the XVIth. century, was completed by their nephew, John Coucher Dent, A.D. 1863."

In the year 1837, John Dent and William Dent, Esqrs., of the city of Worcester, gentlemen of equal liberality and taste, and who had previously purchased the greater part of the Sudeley estates, succeeded in treating with the Duke for the castle and the remainder, and "with a laudable solicitude to rescue from its impending fate so interesting and fine a monument of bygone days,—for which the country owes them a debt of gratitude,—promptly commenced the work of reparation."

PICTON CASTLE,

NEAR HAVERFORDWEST, PEMBROKESHIRE.—PHILLIPS.

FREQUENTLY, as will be seen, as this ancient mansion has changed proprietors, it is said that it has never been without an occupant since the time of its first erection. Altered it has been, as may well be supposed, and added to, and that often, according to the varying tastes of its successive owners, but in its main features it has "braved the battle and the breeze" through all these long centuries. And well may it have been kept to as a dwelling-place in time past, by those who have had taste to enjoy the landscape which is afforded by well-timbered grounds, and the confluence of the two noble streams which form the Haven of Milford.

Picton Castle was a fortified residence before the time of WILLIAM RUFUS.

William de Picton, a Norman Knight, having dispossessed and perhaps slain the original owner of the fortress, established his own family in the succession. After the lapse of several generations the line ended in two brothers—

1. Sir William Picton, and

2. Sir Philip Picton, who married Maud, daughter of William Dyer, of Newport, Pembrokeshire, and was ancestor of the Pictons of Poyston, in that county, of which family was the gallant Sir Thomas Picton.

The elder brother,

Sir William Picton, had a daughter and heiress, who married Sir John Wogan, of Weston, Knight, and brought him Picton Castle as her dowry.

Their descendant,

Sir John Wogan, of Picton Castle, married Anne, daughter of James Butler, Earl of Ormonde, by whom he had two daughters and co-heiresses, namely,

1. Katharine Butler.

2. Anne Butler, married Sir Oliver Eustace, an Irish gentleman.

The elder co-heiress,

KATHARINE BUTLER, married Owen Donn, or Dunn, of Muddlescombe, in Carmarthenshire, and inherited Picton Castle as her marriage portion. They had

HENRY DONN, afterwards Knight, who married Margaret, daughter of Sir Henry Wogan, Knight, of Wiston, the heir of the afore-mentioned, and was killed, together with his brother-in-law Sir Henry Wogan, and others of the Welsh gentry, at the battle of Banbury, in 1469. He left issue two daughters, one of whom,

Jane Donn, married Thomas ap Philip, of Cilsant, in the county of Carmarthen, descended from the princely race of Cadivor ap Collwynn, Lord of Dyved, or Pembrokeshire, who died in 1089, and brought him Picton Castle. He was knighted about the year 1512, and his great grandson,

Sir John Phillips, Knight, was created a Baronet in 1621. He died March 27th., 1629. His son,

Sir Richard Phillips, garrisoned Picton Castle in behalf of the king during the civil wars. It sustained a long siege, and would not have surrendered when it did but for the following circumstance:—In the lower storey of one of the bastions was the nursery, having in it a small window, at which a maid-servant standing with Sir Erasmus Phillips, then an infant, in her arms, when a trooper of the Parliamentary forces approached it on horseback with a flag of truce and a letter; to receive which the girl opened the window, and while she stretched forward, the soldier, lifting himself on his stirrups, snatched the child from her arms, and rode with him into the camp. A message was then forwarded to the governor of the garrison, informing him that unless the Castle was immediately surrendered the child would be put to death. On this the garrison yielded, and was allowed to march out with the honours of war. It is said that the Parliamentary general was so touched by the loyalty of Sir Richard Phillips, and the stratagem by which he had been compelled to surrender, that he gave orders that Picton Castle should not be demolished, as was the fate of the other fortresses of Pembrokeshire. Thus saved, the Castle and domains passed from father to son to the fifth Baronet,

Sir Erasmus Phillips, who was drowned at Bath in 1743, was succeeded in the title and estates by his brother (of Kilgetty) as

Sir John Phillips, who was, in 1776, created BARON MILFORD of the kingdom of Ireland. At his death, issueless, in 1823, the Peerage became extinct, but the Baronetcy passed to the family of Phillips, of Sandy Haven, in the county of Pembrokeshire, in which it still continues.

The Castle and estates of Picton were bequeathed by Lord Milford to

Richard Bulkeley Phillips Grant, Esq., who was great great grandson of Bulkeley Phillips, Esq., of Abercover, in the county of Carmarthen, youngest son of Sir John Phillips, the fourth Baronet. He was created a Baronet in 1828, and a Peer of the Realm in 1847, under the title of

Baron Milford of Picton Castle, in the County of Pembroke. He died January 3rd., 1857, without children, when the Peerage and Baronetcy became extinct, but the Castle and estates passed, under the will of the first Lord Milford, to his half-brother,

The Rev. James Henry Alexander Gwyther, who married Miss Mary Lee, an old friend of the wife of the author of the present work, assumed by Royal license the surname of Phillips, and has issue.

WENTWORTH HOUSE.

WENTWORTH HOUSE,

NEAR ROTHERHAM, YORKSHIRE.—EARL FITZWILLIAM.

———

THIS grand seat of one of our greatest English families is most beautifully situated in the West-Riding of Yorkshire, four miles from "Fair Rotherham"—fair in the days of the "Dragon of Wantley," but I fear me hardly deserving of the name now, for its smoke—nine from Sheffield, and thirteen from Doncaster.

I borrow the following brief description of it from the pen of my obliging friend, Sir Bernard Burke, who has most kindly placed his vast and elaborate stores at my disposal for the use of the present work.

Wentworth House is a magnificent edifice, built by the Marquess of Rockingham, and standing in the midst of a park that presents one of the most beautiful landscapes of the kind to be met with throughout the whole country. The building consists of an irregular quadrangle enclosing three courts, with two grand fronts, the principal one of which, towards the park, consists of a centre, with two wings extending in a line of more than six hundred feet. Before it is a splendid portico sixty feet long, and projecting no less than twenty, which is supported by six handsome Corinthian columns upon pedestals, with a balustrade about the area. Three light figures surmount the pediment, and in the tympanum are the arms and supporters of the Marquess of Rockingham. Statues are also placed at the angles of the centre upon the balustrade, and between them are handsome vases.

The grand hall is sixty feet square, and forty feet in height. A gallery ten feet in width is carried quite round it, being supported by eighteen fluted Ionic pillars, with bases and capitals of white marble, while the shafts are of sienna. In niches between the columns are marble images, above which are medallions, containing relievos from the designs of the celebrated traveller known under the soubriquet of Athenian Stuart. The roof over the gallery is upheld by Corinthian pilasters united by festoons. The ceiling is divided into ornamental compartments.

To the left of this hall are some of the finest apartments of the building, namely, the supper-room, drawing-room, and dining-room. To the left are an ante-room, a grand drawing-room, a dressing-room, and a state bedchamber. In this mansion also is a splendid library, containing many valuable works, and the largest selection, perhaps, of medals to be seen in England.

The park contains fifteen hundred acres, the ground being beautifully varied with noble woods and more than one handsome sheet of water. The aid of architecture has also been called in to heighten the general effect of the landscape by many ornamental temples, that break in upon the eye at every angle.

On an eminence about a mile from the principal front is a monument ninety feet high, erected in 1788 to the memory of the Marquis of Rockingham.

Many exquisite paintings are to be seen here, and among them,—A sleeping Cupid, by Guido; the Death of Lucretia, by Guido; the taking down from the Cross, by Caracci; a Magdalen, by Titian; a Portuguese Female, by Paul Giardano; the Earl of Strafford and his Secretary, by Vandyke, "a very celebrated picture, and generally concluded to be the finest work of that artist;" etc., etc., etc.

The private chapel also contains several very valuable paintings.

The musuem, too, has many valuable and interesting antiques.

———

This family may be traced up to Fitz-Godric, cousin to King Edward the Confessor.

12 AP 66

EVERINGHAM PARK,

EVERINGHAM is one of those homely English mansions which speak to the passer-by of the quiet peacefulness of the "land we live in," and suggest thought of the word "comfort," a word said to be peculiar to our country, and to have no counterpart in any foreign language, the reality in its fulness being only known in Old England.

The house is of red brick, built about the year 1760. It stands at one corner of an extensive deer park, well wooded with ancient oaks and a variety of other trees. Attached to it is a handsome Roman Catholic Chapel, designed after the "Maison Quarrée" at Nismes, in Languedoc.

This park, which is about five miles from Market Weighton, in the East-Riding of Yorkshire, was anciently a domain of the Archbishops of York, and was given about the year 600 to a noble lady named Everilda, or Everildis, afterwards called Saint Everilda. She founded here a large convent, which was called Everildisham after her, and the village feast, as I am informed by Lord Herries, is still held in honour of her name; but the church, I find, is stated in Lawton's "Collectio rerum Ecclesiasticarum," to be dedicated to Saint Emeldis.

The church, in which was a chantry, was in the patronage of the Everinghams, and the estate came from them to the Elleys, next to the Suthills, and lastly to the Constables, of Flamborough, by the marriage of the heiress of John Suthill, Esq., with Sir Marmaduke Constable.

The town of Everingham was held by the family of Everingham, (namely, half a knight's fee or the manor,) of the fee of the Archbishop of York, by the service of performing the office of butler in his house upon the day of his enthronization; and two carucates of land were held of the fee of Lincoln, and paid nine shillings to the Sheriff's fine.

At the time of the Survey the manor was held by the Archbishop of York.

The principal paintings are:—Sir Thomas More, by Holbein; An Alchemist, by P. Teniers; Pope Sixtus Quintus; Lady Lucy Herbert; Lady Constable, by Sir Peter Lely; Venice, by Canaletti; and two sea pieces by Vernet, with several others.

In the library are some interesting old manuscript works formerly belonging to St. Mary's Abbey, York, and other abbeys of Yorkshire.

The family of Lord Herries derives paternally from Thomas Haggerston, Esq., of Haggerston Castle, in the county of Northumberland, Commanding Officer of a regiment in the service of King Charles I., who was created a Baronet on the 15th. of August, 1643.

His Lordship represents in the female line the families of Maxwell, of Carlaverock, Earls of Nithsdale, and Constable, of Everingham.

HOLME LACY.

HOLME LACY,

NEAR HEREFORD, HEREFORDSHIRE.—STANHOPE, BARONET.

MANY as are the seats in fair England, to each and every one of which the words of Spenser are so justly applicable,—

> "There the most daintie paradise on ground
> Itself doth offer to the sober eye,
> In which all pleasures plenteously abound,
> And none does others happiness envye.
> The painted flowers; the trees upshooting hye;
> The dales for shade; the hilles for breathing space;
> The trembling groves; the christall running by;
> And that which all fair works doth most aggrace,
> The art which all that wrought appeared in no place;"

there are few that surpass Holme Lacy in the exceeding beauty of its situation.

The name Holme is otherwise written Hamme, the Saxon word for a house, farm, or village; also, sometimes, Home, Hom, or Homme, meaning a place surrounded by water. The additional name of Lacy was derived to it from Walter de Lacy, a valiant Norman, who soon after the Conquest obtained vast possessions in the county of Hereford, so much so, that in the reign of William Rufus his son Roger had no fewer than sixty-five lordships in the county, of which the principal one was Holme.

So much for the place; now for the persons.

The ancient family of Scudamore was one of those whose names were inscribed on the Roll of Battle Abbey, and after living in high esteem in the county of Hereford for centuries,

JOHN SCUDAMORE, of Holme Lacy, was High Sheriff of the County in the 16th., 21st., and 35th. years of the reign of King Henry VIII. He married Sybil, daughter of Watkin Vaughan, of Hengist, lived to a great age, and was buried, with his wife, in the church of the parish, where there is a fine old monument of their two recumbent figures in alabaster.

The representative in the sixteenth century was

WILLIAM SCUDAMORE, who was Gentleman Usher to Queen Elizabeth, Standard-bearer to the Honourable Board of Gentlemen Pensioners, and one of Her Majesty's Council for the Marches of Wales. He was Member of Parliament for the Shire in five successive Parliaments, and High Sheriff for the County in 1581. He was a great benefactor to the Bodleian Library at Oxford, and his son, Sir James Scudamore, was another of the chiefest friends of the justly celebrated Sir Thomas Bodley. Sir

William was knighted for his signal bravery at the siege of Cadiz, and served in Parliament for the county of Hereford in the first year of the reign of King James I. He was one of the most renowned men in England for chivalry, and no more need be said of him than that he is the "Sir Scudamore" of Spenser's "Faerie Queene." He married Ursula, daughter and co-heiress of Sir John Pakington, of Westwood Park, in Worcestershire, and had issue,

     1. John, of whom presently.

     2. Barnabas.

The younger son, Barnabas, was in the army of King Charles I., and Governor of Hereford, which city he stoutly defended against the Scottish army under the Earl of Leven. He was twice summoned to surrender, but the following letter was his spirited reply.

     "My Lord,

          "I am not to give up the King's garrison upon any summons or letter; neither shall it be in the power of the Mayor or other to condescend to any such proposition made unto him. I was set in here by the King's command, and shall not quit it but by special order from His Majesty or the Prince; and with this resolution I shall persist in Hereford.

     "This last day of July, 1645.

                           "BARNABAS SCUDAMORE."

His refusal prolonged the siege for another fortnight, but the city gallantly held out, and at the end of that time a second and similar demand was sent by the Earl, to which the knight replied as follows:—

     "My Lord,

          "For your favourable proffer to the inhabitants of this city, I shall returne their thankes, and resolution that they intend to suffer with me, and I shall not suffer alone for the suffusion of bloud. I am sorry to think of it, that two united nations should so much differ, having paid once well for Scotland's friendship. My Lord, I am resolved to endure all ruines and stormes which shall be made against this place, and doubt not, by God's assistance, to render His Majestie a good account of it; the which by my endeavours I shall maintain to the last, and remaine

                    "Your Lordship's Servant,

                           "BARNABAS SCUDAMORE."

"To the Right Honourable the Earl of Leven, General of the Scottish Forces."

In consequence of this firm conduct, a general assault was determined on by the besiegers, but on the appearance of the king from Worcester, with a superior force, the Scots suddenly broke up, and dispersed. It appears, from the "Iter Carolinum," that the king thereupon supped and slept at Holme Lacy.

The eldest son,

JOHN SCUDAMORE, was created a Baronet in 1620, in which year he was elected

Member for the County, and in 1628 was raised to the dignity of Baron of Dromore and Viscount Scudamore of Sligo, in the Peerage of Ireland. In 1634 he was sent Ambassador to the Court of France, in which office he acquitted himself with great dignity and discretion.

After three more generations the male line ended, when the titles of Baronet, Baron, and Viscount became extinct, and the estates devolved upon

Sir Edwyn Francis Scudamore Stanhope, Bart., as lineal descendant of Mary, (wife of Sir Giles Brydges, of Wilton Castle, Herefordshire,) daughter of Sir James Scudamore, Knight, and sister of John, first Viscount Scudamore.

The original mansion of Holme Lacy is supposed to have been built by John Scudamore, Esq., at the latter end of the reign of Henry VIII., the letters E P, with the badges of the Prince of Wales, afterwards King Edward VI., in painted glass, being found in the old house. It was partly rebuilt in the reign of William III. by John, Viscount Scudamore, but has only recently been completed.

"The house presents an uniform structure, nearly in the shape of the letter H, having three fronts of stone, with projecting wings. The north and east fronts are nearly two hundred feet in length, and the south front one hundred and fifty feet. The house is approached by a noble terrace, seven hundred feet long, and forty-seven feet wide. The entrance-hall opens upon a gallery ninety feet in length, and is lighted by five windows of stained glass, in which are the arms of Brydges, Scudamore, and Stanhope. At the further end of the gallery, folding doors open upon the principal staircase, lighted by a large window of painted glass, in which are the arms of King Henry VIII and Edward, Prince of Wales. On the left side of the gallery, doors open into the principal apartments, which are lofty and well proportioned, having richly stuccoed ceilings in compartments of flowers and various other designs, especially the saloon, a room of spacious dimensions, thirty-one feet in height, the ceiling of which is of most beautiful design, having pendant festoons of fruit and flowers; also some fine carving by Grinling Gibbons, over the chimney-piece. In this room and the dining-room adjoining are some fine family portraits by Vandyke, Sir Peter Lely, and others. The whole of the rooms on the ground-floor are of good proportion, and communicate with one another by folding doors, to the length of one hundred and thirty feet, and other rooms on the right and left. In these rooms are some exquisite specimens of carving by the celebrated Grinling Gibbons, in bird, shell-fish, fruit, flowers, etc.

The gardens and pleasure-grounds of Holme Lacy are extensive and unique, particularly those on the south side, which are laid out in King William's style of fortification, with magnificent yew hedges of extraordinary height and thickness. The flower-garden, which is modern, is extremely beautiful. On the south side is also a terrace, eight hundred feet in length by thirty feet wide, communicating with other terraces and walks of lesser extent.

Pope, Gay, and other *literati* of that day, were much at Holme Lacy during the time of the last Lady Scudamore, and often spent their summers with that lady. It was at Holme Lacy Pope became acquainted with John Kyrle, whom he has celebrated under the title of "The Man of Ross," a poem he wrote at Holme Lacy.

In the garden of the Vicarage-house at Holme Lacy is a remarkable pear tree, which formerly covered nearly an acre of ground; much of it has, however, been cut down from time to time, owing to its too closely surrounding the house. From fourteen to sixteen hogsheads of perry, of one hundred gallons each, have been made from this tree in one year. In its growth, it in some sort resembles the growth of the banyan tree.

The scenery around Holme Lacy is highly picturesque, and replete with endless variety. The view from the east end of the south terrace is surpassingly beautiful. The old tower of Holme Lacy church, with the spire of Fownhope on the right, the hills of Fownhope, richly wooded from the summit to the base; Caplar Hill, on the top of which are the remains of a Roman camp, with the Wye running at its base, form altogether a landscape rarely equalled. The scene is again charmingly varied as you ascend the park, (well stocked with deer,) which takes in other agreeable objects, and more of the Wye's meandering river. Still further on the distant view expands nobly, whilst the huge and magnificent oaks, those venerable giants of the forests, spread their umbrageous arms everywhere around. From the summit of this beautiful park you command the Black Mountains, in Brecknockshire; the Clee Hills, in Shropshire; the celebrated Malvern Hills, in Worcestershire; and the well-known hills called "Robin Hood's Butts."

Although there are, doubtless, many seats more important from historical recollections and associations, few surpass Holme Lacy in beauty of situation and surrounding scenery."

EATON HALL,

NEAR CHESTER, CHESHIRE.—MARQUIS OF WESTMINSTER.

IN the reign of Henry III. the manor of Eton was possessed by Hamon de Pulford, whose son

RICHARD took his name of ETON from the place itself, and it continued with his descendants, the Etons, till after the death of

JOHN ETON, whose daughter and heiress,

JOAN ETON, by her marriage with Ralph, second son of Sir Thomas Grosvenor, conveyed it into the family of the present owner.

At the close of the last century Eaton Hall was a heavy brick mansion, built by the architect Sir John Vanbrugh, on whom the sarcastic epitaph was written,

> "Lie heavy on him, earth, for he
> Laid many a heavy load on thee."

The gardens, too, were formed on a corresponding model, diversified with straight walks and leaden statues.

In the year 1803, the whole, with the exception of the basement storey, was pulled down by the then Marquis of Westminster, and the present pile erected in its stead, but owing to its great size and ornamented character, several years elapsed before it was finished, and it was not till 1825 that the main building was completed. It consists of a centre and two wings, each differing in design from the other.

In the middle of the west front is a large portico, sustained by clusters of columns, under which there is a carriage-way to the steps before the principal entrance-hall.

The eastern front has a cloister along its whole length, and leads to a terrace three hundred and fifty feet long, from which an admirable view of the grounds and neighbouring country is obtained.

The grand entrance-hall is forty-one feet long by thirty-one feet wide, and is two storeys in height.

The dining-room is fifty feet long by thirty-seven feet wide, and contains several statues and valuable pictures.

The ante-drawing-room is painted in arabesque.

The drawing-room is of the same form as the dining-room, namely, fifty feet long and thirty-seven feet wide, and contains also many paintings of value.

The library is one hundred and twenty feet long, but of different degrees of width, and from it the view through the corridor to the further end of the house is a distance of four hundred and seventy-two feet. The book-cases in it are of carved oak, and contain many very valuable manuscripts, and a large portion of the famous lost record denominated "The Cheshire Domesday."

The great staircase, state apartments, and the tenants' hall, are all of corresponding size and ornamentation.

The flower gardens cover full fifty acres of ground, and they, too, when the house was pulled down, received the like share of alteration and improvement.

The principal entrance is through the Chester Gateway, an imposing structure.

The views in the neighbourhood are very fine, embracing towards the west the Welsh mountains; towards the east the Peckforton Hills, with the crag on which stands the ruins of Beeston Castle; on the south the Dee follows its winding course, the gardens sloping down to its bank; and at the distance of a mile and a half the parish church of Eccleston, a beautiful Gothic building, adds the last feature, which may be said to be wanting to no country house in England.

There is a large collection of valuable pictures, among which are,—Our Saviour on the Mount of Olives, by Claude Lorraine, said to be the largest picture ever painted by that artist; A View of the Mediterranean, by Vernet; David and Abigail, by Rubens; Rubens and his second Wife, by himself.

———

The family of Grosvenor is of French extraction, and is stated to be composed of the words "gross" and "veneur." It deduces from Gilbert Le Grosvenor, a companion of the Norman William I.

THORYBERGH PARK.

THRYBERGH PARK,

THRYBERGH PARK is very pleasantly situated in the West-Riding of Yorkshire, about three miles from the town of Rotherham.

At a remote period the estate of Thrybergh belonged to William de Perci, the founder of the great house of Percy.

It afterwards came into possession of the Reresbys.

The old Hall of the Reresbys, which was also retained during the possession of the families of Savile and Finch, with alterations from time to time, was pulled down by Colonel Fullerton, and the present handsome Gothic edifice erected in its stead.

The ancient and eminent family of Reresby was settled here from the time of the Conquest.

SIR ADAM RERESBY, Knight, was followed by sixteen successors in the direct male line, when

SIR JOHN RERESBY, Knight, of Thrybergh, Governor of Hull, was created a Baronet by King Charles I., 16th. of May, 1642. He married Frances, daughter of Edmund Yarburgh, Esq., of Balne Hall, Yorkshire, and died in April, 1646, when their eldest son,

SIR JOHN RERESBY, of Thrybergh, Governor of York, succeeded. He married Frances, daughter of William Brown, Esq. of York, and had, with other issue, a son, who, at his father's death, in May, 1689, inherited the Baronetcy, and became

SIR WILLIAM RERESBY, BART., a person of profligate and worthless character, who, so far from following in the steps of his distinguished father, exhibited only a melancholy contrast to it. Hunter the historian has left the following record of him:—"In 1705 he had sold Thrybergh and the estates connected with it. He was alive in 1727, when Wotton's account of the Baronets was published. In that work he is said to be reduced to a low condition. Brooke was informed that he was tapster of the Fleet Prison. This is not improbable, for his tastes and habits appear to have been of the lowest order. I have seen one sad evidence. He died in great obscurity, a melancholy instance how low pursuits and base pleasures may sully the noblest name, and waste an estate, gathered with labour, and preserved with care by a race of distinguished ancestors. Gaming was amongst his follies, and particularly that lowest specimen of the folly, the fights of game cocks. The tradition at Thrybergh is, for his name is not quite forgotten, that the estate of Dennaby was staked and lost on a single main." He died, fortunately, unmarried, when the Baronetcy, in all probability an empty honour, after the squandering of the property to the amount of seventeen thousand a year, devolved on his brother,

SIR LEONARD RERESBY, fourth Baronet, who died unmarried on the 11th. of August, 1748, when the Baronetcy expired.

Thrybergh had been sold by Sir William to

JOHN SAVILE, ESQ., of Methley, near Leeds, whose granddaughter,

ELIZABETH SAVILE, married

THE HON. JOHN FINCH, Earl of Aylesford, and was succeeded by her son,

SAVILE FINCH, ESQ., of Thrybergh, who, having no son, left the estates to his wife Judith, daughter of John Fullerton, Esq., by whom they were bequeathed to her own family.

The family of Fullerton is of Scotch origin, and is descended from Allan Fullerton of that ilk, living in 1240.

FLEURS CASTLE.

FLEURS CASTLE,

NEAR KELSO, ROXBURGHSHIRE.—DUKE OF ROXBURGHE.

HAVING seen more or less of some of the Seats which I have already briefly described, as well as of many others, there is none which struck me, when I saw it some years ago, as more beautifully situated than the grand ducal residence of Fleurs, which I had frequent opportunities of admiring when on a salmon-fishing expedition to the Tweed. The kind friend who had invited me to stay a fortnight with him and his family at Kelso, on their way back from a tour in Scotland, is now no more, but all the recollections of a very pleasant visit still remain, and as they were lodging at the house of the Duke's steward, which was close to the Park grounds, I saw the place to every advantage.

It was anciently called Floors, the name derived, it is said, from its standing on a natural floor or terrace, overlooking a plain of extensive meadowland, which reaches down to the Tweed, at the spot where the Teviot joins it, both rivers then in one winding beautifully through the estate directly in front of the house, till they flow together under Kelso bridge, a noble stream of water, the very home of the salmon after his journey to the sea.

To the south is a lovely view, embracing a prospect of eight or nine miles over Teviotdale, a rich and picturesque valley, worthy of its poet, Sir Walter Scott, and the scene is bounded by the lofty eminences of the Cheviot Hills and the "Border Land" of Northumberland.

In this Park King James the II. of Scotland met his death by mischance, through the bursting of a cannon, while engaged in superintending the siege of the Castle opposite, and a holly tree, enclosed within rails, still marks the spot where the catastrophe occurred. His successor, James III., was proclaimed King, and crowned with military pomp a few days afterwards, in the neighbouring town of Kelso.

The house, which is a magnificent pile of building, was erected in the year 1718, by John, first Duke of Roxburghe.

It contains pictures by Vandyke, Lely, Reynolds, Raeburn, Ramsay, Fratoni, etc.

John, the third Duke, who succeeded to the title in 1755, collected a rare library of old English literature, especially in the department of the Drama, and at its sale, in 1812, the literary society known by the name of the Roxburghe Club was established in memorial of this valuable collection.

Fleurs Castle was honoured with a visit from their Royal Highnesses the Prince and Princess of Wales at the latter end of the year 1865.

————

The ducal family of Roxburghe derives from Sir James Innes, Bart., of Innes, who married Margaret, third daughter of William, Lord Ker, second and surviving son of Sir Robert Ker, of Cessford, created Lord Roxburghe in 1600, and Baron Ker of Cessford and Cavertown, Earl of Roxburghe, in 1666.

Of the family of Innes, it is stated by Duncan Forbes, in a MS. account, that in all their long line "their inheritance never went to a woman; that none of them ever married an ill wife; and that no friends ever suffered for their debts."

LEA,

LEA shortly after the Conquest was possessed by the family of Trehamton, of whom the first we find was

GALFRIDUS DE TREHAMTON *tempore* STEPHEN. From him descended

SIR RANULPHUS DE TREHAMTON, who married Joan de Dive. Their daughter Margaret married

JOHN DE BRAOSE.

Sir Ranulph was Member for the County of Lincoln, *temp.* Edward I., and sat in the Parliament which assembled at Rhudlan, in Wales. His effigy in chain armour is in Lea Church.

The Manor of Lea went, by the marriage of Agnes de Braose to Urian St. Pierre, to the Cokesays, Grevilles, Berkeleys, and Howards, was bought by the Dalisons, *temp.* Edward VI., and again sold to their kinsman, Sir Edmund Anderson, of Broughton, *temp.* Elizabeth, and it is somewhat remarkable that by the marriage of Sir William Anderson with Anne Maddison their descendants get the Trehamton blood, through the Bosviles, Barnbys, Nuthills, and De Braoses, from which families the Maddisons lineally descend.

The old residence at Lea was a moated Manor House, a mile to the east of the church, of which only the moats and fishponds remain. A handsome gold ring with the figures of St. Mary and St. Anne upon it, was dug up there a few years ago, being a lady of quality's ring of about Henry VI.'s time, and is preserved.

The present Hall is an old farm-house added to since the family removed out of Yorkshire, and has nothing of particular interest about it, except an old chimney-piece, some oak panelling, and some family portraits, namely,—Sir Edmund Anderson, Knight, Chief Justice of the Common Pleas, *temp.* Elizabeth, on panel; Lord Sheffield of Boterwoke, on panel; John Sheffield, Earl of Mulgrave, by Sir Godfrey Kneller; Mr. Darley, of Aldby Park, by Sir Joshua Reynolds; Sir John Lawrence, Lord Mayor of London in the year of the plague, by Soest; Sir J. Nelthorpe, by Sir Thomas Lawrence; and others of only family interest.

The skirmish between the Royalists and Parliamentarians, in which Colonel Cavendish was slain, began in Lea parish, where two fields, the "Graves Close" and "Redcoats," still attest the fact.

Henry VIII. and Katherine Howard passed through Lea in their progress towards Yorkshire, and spent two days at Lord Burgh's house at Gainsborough.

––––––––

The family of Anderson, Baronet, of Yorkshire and Lincolnshire, is stated to derive from the L'Isles of Northumberland, one of that family, Robert L'Isle, in the reign of Henry IV., marrying an heiress of the house of Anderson.

FARNHAM HOUSE.

FARNHAM HOUSE,

THE only drawback that I have experienced in placing before my readers these views of English Homes and Home Scenery, the great ornaments of the country, which, as they have so often and so much pleased myself, and still please even in thus recalling, will, it is hoped, give somewhat of the like pleasure to others, is, that only one view of each country seat can be given, when an almost unlimited variety might as well, or almost equally as well, be represented. How much this remark applies to the one at present before us, may readily be understood from the fact that it stands in grounds, the various drives through which extend to no less than twenty-six miles, the demesne itself richly planted and of an undulating character, and containing four lakes, with a range of mountains in the distance, extending from Florence Court, the seat of the Earl of Enniskillen, away towards Sligo. The deer park contains three hundred head of deer. The woods are planted with fine beech trees, said to be the first planted in Ireland: and one of them, Derigid Wood, dating from 1642, is said to be the finest oak wood in that kingdom.

The estate was granted by King James I. to Sir Richard Waldron, of Leicestershire, who married Miss Farnham of the same county, and gave her name to the property, and it was purchased shortly after 1641 by Robert Maxwell, Bishop of Kilmore, lineal ancestor of the present Lord Farnham, and the immediate successor of the celebrated Bishop Bedell.

The house was built in the year 1700, and considerably enlarged in 1803, and further improved in 1839.

It contains a very valuable and extensive library in all departments of literature, with illustrated works, prints, and drawings.

The Museum has a splendid collection of minerals and geological specimens, as also antiquities from Pompeii, Herculaneum, and the ancient Etruscan cities, Roman cameos, Mosaics, and a large variety of other articles of *vertù*.

The hothouses, greenhouses, and conservatory are rich in the rarest varieties of exotic and other plants.

Among the valuable collection of paintings are the following:—The Miracle of the Loaves and Fishes, by Tintoretto; The Washing the Disciples' Feet, by Tintoretto; A Pilgrim in the Desert, by Guercino; Barry, second Earl of Farnham, by Opie; Robert, first Earl of Farnham, by Slaughter, Sergeant Painter to George II.; The Honourable Mrs. Maxwell, sister to Lord Oriel, (better known as Mr. Foster, Speaker of the Irish House of Commons,) with her eldest son, John, fifth Lord Farnham, by

Angelica Kauffman; Two Landscapes, by Zuccherelli; Autumn, by Clinchet;* Winter, by Clinchet;* View from the Cassina at Florence, by Burzi; View of the Piazza Granduca at Florence, by Burzi; Summer, by Clinchet;* Spring, by Clinchet;* Young Man and Girl Laughing, by Müller, of Munich; A Nun taking the Veil, by Bruls; View of the Bay of Naples, by Marinoni; miniatures on ivory of Martin Luther and his wife, Catherine de Bora, in an ancient carved wood frame; Two Cattle pieces, by Verboeckhoven; View of Amalfi and the Gulf of Salerno, in oil, by Thöming; The Blue Cave, on copper, by Thöming; Italian Woman and Child, by Maes; Adoration of the Magi, on glass, by Bassano; An Original Sketch, by Salvator Rosa; Fruit piece, by Bembi; The Madonna, an original of the school of Guido; Landscape, by Teniers; William III. on Horseback, in the Field of Battle, by Gaspar Netscher; A sketch, by Guardi; View of the Patriarchal Church of Castello, near Venice, by Guardi; View of the Church of Santa Maria della Salute, at Venice, by Guardi; View of the Piazzetta, at Venice, by Guardi; View of the Doge's Palace at Venice, by Guardi; Two Views of La Zuecca, by Guardi; Side View of the Church of SS. Giovanni e Paolo at Venice, by Guardi; View of the Church in "the Lagunes of Venice," called "La Barcetta," by Guardi; View of the Court of the Doge's Palace at Venice, by Guardi; Portrait of William III., by Gaspar Netscher; Helena Forman, the second wife of Rubens, by Rubens; Landscape, by Gaspar Poussin; Copy of the celebrated Marina of Claude Lorraine, in the Galleria degli Uffiz, Florence, by Signorini: this Copy, from its intrinsic merit, received the premium at Florence, among all the exhibited works of living artists, (being dealt with as an original,) the year before Lord Farnham purchased it. John the Baptist with a Lamb, by Jordaens; Landscape, by Gaspar Poussin; An Angel, by Guido Reni; Snow Piece, by Molenaer; The Annunciation, by Carlo Maratti; Landscape, with a Man watering Horses, by Wouvermans; An ancient Copy of the "Madonna della Seggiola," of Raphael, by Ciniani; Landscape, of the School of Salvator Rosa; Three of the Apostles, painted on copper, of the School of Salvator Rosa; Landscape, by Zuccherelli; A Holy Family, by Solimena; Two Landscapes, with Figures, by Bout and Boudwyne; The Sick Lady, by Gaspar Netscher; Landscape, with Cattle, by Zuccherelli; St. John the Evangelist, by Carlo Dolce; View of Amalfi and the Gulf of Salerno, by Thöming; St. Cecilia, by Domenichino; View of the Bay of Naples, by Thöming.

There are besides a large number of very beautiful and valuable paintings and drawings in colour by foreign and other modern artists.

The family of Lord Farnham derives from the second son of Sir John Maxwell, of Calderwood, in Scotland, who went over to Ireland in the interest of King James VI. of that kingdom. His Lordship is also twelfth in descent from King Henry VII., through the houses of Brandon, Seymour, Boyle, and Butler.

---

* These four pictures of "The Seasons," by Clinchet, formed part of the Strawberry Hill Collection, and were presented by the French Ambassador at Rome to Horace Walpole when a youth.

ILAM HALL.

ILAM HALL,

NEAR ASHBOURNE, STAFFORDSHIRE.—WATTS-RUSSELL.

THE situation of Ilam Hall is extremely beautiful, and the house itself is well adapted to the scenery which surrounds it. The old mansion was standing in the year 1820, but was soon afterwards pulled down, and the present fine Elizabethan edifice erected in its place.

There are two streams, the Manifold and the Hamps, which for some miles previously have followed a subterranean course. The following is the account given of them by Rhodes:—"Returning from the meadows to the garden-grounds of Ilam, I passed a narrow foot-bridge at the base of a rocky bank, from whence the two subterranean streams, the Hamps and the Manifold, emerge, and form a river at a burst. This is one of the curiosities of this romantic place. The river Manifold formerly flowed beneath the amphitheatrical sweep of wood that forms the background of Ilam Hall; but it has abandoned its ancient course, where it had continued to run for ages, and now pursues its way for the space of five or six miles through caverns deep in the mountains, where it has obtained a passage to its forsaken channel, which it again enters in the gardens at Ilam. Here the united rivers become a powerful stream, which, within a few yards of the place where they first appear, is precipitated over an artificial barrier, when it forms a cascade of considerable extent and great beauty. The Manifold now becomes a busy and brilliant stream, which, after winding round a part of the village about a quarter of a mile from the principal front of the Hall, flows through some pleasant meadows, and enters the Dove at a short distance from Thorpe Cloud."

The Vale of Ilam is of singular beauty, thus described by the tourist,—"I felt as if I had been treading on fairy-ground; the parts were so beautiful and so exquisitely combined, and the whole so rare and unexpected that it seemed more like a scene of enchantment that might soon pass away than anything real and permanent." "A village of a few houses only scattered amongst trees, a country church with a tower nearly covered with ivy, verdant meadows watered by a busy stream, everywhere sparkling with light, and on a gentle eminence a venerable mansion—the old Hall—rising out of, and backed by, luxuriant foliage, are the principal features of this lovely spot, which is one of the most romantic little vales that nature ever formed. No glen in the Alps was ever more beautiful, more picturesque, or more retired."

Here Congreve wrote the "Old Bachelor" and part of the "Mourning Bride."

Within the house, in addition to the library and music-room, is a picture-gallery eighty feet long, containing, besides other valuable articles, many fine models of ancient ruins, among which may be named—Remains of the Sepulchre of Scipio Africanus, Ruins of part of the Ancient Walls of Rome, Temple of Minerva Medica, Temple of Peace, The Sepulchre of Cæcilia Metella in the Court of the Farnese Palace at Rome, The Temple of Vesta at Tivoli, The Sepulchre of the Horatii and Curiatii at Albana, The Temple of Janus, etc.

In the dining-room is a massive silver candelabrum, presented to Mr. Watts-Russell by the Conservatives of North Staffordshire, in 1834. Its principal ornament, however, is the "Font" of Raphael, originally in the Florence Gallery. It was thus described by the late Noel Jennings, Esq.:—"The magnificent lawn of an oval form, with a recurved edge and pointed bottom, which, as well as the raised zone on the belt, encircles the middle of the outside, is wrought in fluted or gadrooned work. Each side is ornamented with a laughing cornuted satyr's head; two grotesque sphinx-like figures, half satyr and half dragon, with each a double tail, serve as supporters; their arms are extended to the edge, and their hind parts with wings expanded underneath, resting in an oval base which has a hollow gadrooned edge. The whole is painted in the most lively colours, and glazed. On the inside, within a grotesque border, is represented a Roman naval engagement. The boarding of two ships by a number of soldiers in boats, sword and shield in hand; sailors fixing their grappling-hooks to facilitate the entrance of the assailants, who are opposed by soldiers on board the ships, armed in like manner. The exterior is enriched with grotesque figures, supporting festoons and flowers, interspersed among which are birds, military achievements, foliage, etc."

The family before us descends in the male line from John Russell, Esq., of Newcastle-under-Lyme, in Staffordshire, born 1699, whose grandson, Jesse Watts-Russell, Esq., of Worcester College, and Honorary D.C.L. of the University of Oxford, assumed by royal license the additional surname of Watts, before and in addition to his patronymic, quartering also the arms of Watts with those of Russell.

WARWICK CASTLE.

WARWICK CASTLE,

NEAR WARWICK, WARWICKSHIRE.—EARL OF WARWICK.

———————

CYMBELINE, King of Britain, is by some supposed to have built the first stronghold that existed on the site of the grand and historic pile of Warwick Castle.

The Romans have had its original foundation assigned to them by others.

Ethelfleda, a daughter of Alfred the Great, is yet again considered by other antiquarians to have been the foundress of the first Castle that was built here, but however that may be, it seems to be understood that in the year 915 she caused the donjon to be made, which was a strong tower or platform upon a large and high mound of earth, artificially raised—such being usually placed towards the side of a castle or fort which is least defensible.

William the Conqueror bestowed the place upon one of his followers, named

HENRY DE NEWBURGH, whom he at the same time created Earl of Warwick. It next passed to one of the family of

BEAUCHAMP. The last female heir of that line conveyed it by her marriage to the celebrated

RICHARD NEVILLE, the "King Maker," who assumed the title of Earl of Warwick. Upon his decease, his daughter having married the Duke of Clarence, the latter was allowed by the King, Edward IV., to take the vacant dignity. The Castle was much strengthened and ornamented by him, but upon his forfeiture it was granted to the family of

DUDLEY, during whose possession of the seat it was visited by Queen Elizabeth in one of her "progresses," and the following somewhat characteristic story relative to the event is related of Her Majesty;

"The bailief, rising out of the place where he knelid, approchid nere to the coche or chariott wherin her Maiestie satt, and coming to the side thereof, kneling downe, offered unto her Maiestie a purse very faire vrought, and in the purse twenty pounds, all in sovereignes, which her Maiestie putting furth her hand recevid, showing withall a very benign and gracious countenance." "And therewithall offered her hand to the bailief to kisse, who kissed it, and then she deliverid to him agayne his mase, which she kept on her lappe all the tyme of the oracyon. And after the mase deliverid, she called Mr. Aglionby to her, and offered her hand to him to kisse, withall smyling said, 'Come hither, little recorder; it was told me that youe wold be afraid to look upon me or to speake boldly; but youe were not so afraid of me as I was of youe.'"

On the failure of the line of Dudley, the earldom was bestowed by King James on ROBERT, LORD RICH, but the castle he gave to

SIR FULKE GREVILLE, afterwards Lord Brooke, who, Dugdale says, laid out no less than £20,000, a vast sum in those days, on its improvement. His successor,

LORD BROOKE, was a rigid Parliamentarian, and fortified his castle on their behalf; but, advancing upon Lichfield, which was held by a strong force of Royalists for the King, he was shot dead by a soldier from a wall. His descendant,

FRANCIS GREVILLE, was created Earl of Warwick in 1747, and was ancestor of the present possessor.

The approach to Warwick Castle is through an embattled gateway at the entrance of the town. The road is cut through a solid rock, overgrown with moss and ivy, and crowned with trees and shrubs of various kinds, winding along for nearly a quarter of a mile, when the noble building breaks at once upon the sight in all its magnificence. On the right hand is *Guy's Tower*, the walls of which are ten feet thick and one hundred and twenty-eight feet high. Upon the left is a pile called *Cæsar's Tower*, connected with the former by a strong wall, in the centre of which is a ponderous gateway with a portcullis, leading to the inner court.

The entrance-hall is sixty feet long and forty feet broad, reaching to the very roof of the castle. Its walls are characteristically covered with ancient armour—swords, shields, helmets, spears, and the like—strongly recalling the idea of olden times. Adjoining the hall is a dining-room, more modern than any other part of the building. Beyond this again, is a magnificent suite of state apartments, consisting of two state drawing-rooms and a boudoir, and other apartments.

The walls are adorned with a series of valuable paintings by the old masters, among which are the famous paintings of Charles the First on horseback by Vandyke, and the portrait of Ignatius Loyola by Rubens.

In the greenhouse is the celebrated "Warwick Vase" of white marble, twenty-one feet in circumference, and seven in diameter, discovered in the baths of the Emperor Adrian, presented by the Queen of Naples to Sir William Hamilton, who gave it to the Earl of Warwick.

There is also the magnificent "Kenilworth Buffet," presented to Lord Brooke on his marriage by his friends in the county, of which it was to be a memorial heir-loom in the castle.

———

The family of Greville descends from William Greville, a citizen of London, living in the year 1397.

BURTON CONSTABLE,

NEAR KINGSTON-UPON-HULL, YORKSHIRE.—CONSTABLE, BARONET.

THE fine old baronial seat of Burton Constable is situated in Holderness, in the East-Riding of Yorkshire, about nine miles from the town of Kingston-upon-Hull, and brings before our minds at once the "olden times," when,

> "In rough magnificence array'd,
> Our ancient chivalry display'd
> The pomp of her heroic games,
> And crested chiefs and tissued dames
> Assembled at the clarion's call
> In some proud castle's high-arch'd hall."

The spacious park contains a fine piece of water, crossed at one part by an ornamental bridge, over which the road leads to the porter's lodge.

The house, which is supposed to have been in the first instance built in the reign of King Stephen, has two fronts, the one towards the west one hundred and ninety-one feet long, and the other towards the east one hundred and thirty-three feet, the remainder of the equivalent length being filled up by two projecting wings, each seventy-eight feet long, and four square battlemented towers rise a little above the level of the roof at either end of the main building.

The inside of this fine house is in keeping with its outside appearance. .There is a gallery one hundred and thirteen feet long and nineteen feet high, its walls adorned with a series of family paintings, and containing also a great variety of valuable mathematical instruments.

The entrance-hall is sixty feet in length, thirty-one feet wide, and of the like height.

The library is also of large size, and well furnished with a valuable collection of books.

Among the miscellaneous curiosities are four beautiful tables of black marble, richly inlaid with various colours, the handiwork of Italian artists.

This family derives in the paternal line from Richard Fitz Pont, whose son Walter, living in the reign of Henry the Second, married Margaret, daughter and heiress of

Ralph de Todeni, with whom he acquired Clifford Castle, in Herefordshire, and thence assumed the name of Clifford. He had issue, two sons, of whom the elder was,

WALTER DE CLIFFORD, whose great grandson,

ROGER DE CLIFFORD, was renowned for his valour in the wars of HENRY the Third, and EDWARD the First. He married Isabel, eldest daughter and coheiress of Roger de Vipont, Lord of Westmoreland. He fell in the Welsh war, in the year 1282. Some generations after him,

SIR LEWIS DE CLIFFORD, K.G., was distinguished in the reigns of EDWARD the Third, RICHARD the Second, and HENRY the Fourth. His descendant,

THOMAS HUGH CLIFFORD, created a Baronet in the year 1814, assumed by Royal Licence the name of Constable, and was ancestor of the present family.

FRANKS

FRANKS,

THIS place is situated in the parish of Horton Kirby, near Farningham, in the county of Kent.

It belonged in Henry the Third's time to a family of the same name, Frank, or Franks, which came out of Yorkshire and settled here.

This name, sometimes written Frankish, in Henry the Sixth's time was changed to that of Martin, and continued with the same till the reign of Queen Elizabeth, when it was sold to

LANCELOT BATHURST, alderman of the City of London, who pulled down the house, which was then situated on the right side of the river Darenth, and built a magnificent seat on the opposite bank, which in Philpott's time was in possession of

SIR EDWARD BATHURST, and continued in his line till the beginning of the present century, when the estate was purchased by a person of the name of

RAY, and continued in that family till the year 1860, when it was bought, being then almost a ruin, by

ROBERT BRADFORD, ESQ., who took down a great part of the interior, and restored it (as nearly as possible) to its pristine state.

Queen Elizabeth used frequently to stay at this place when it was in the possession of the Bathursts, and there are now two rooms in the house which are called Queen Elizabeth's rooms, and some of the fine old ceiling and panelling are preserved.

The river Darenth, which flows close by the house, is famous for its excellent trout fishing. Darenth Wood has also long been noted by entomologists as an excellent hunting-ground.

This is one of these families, so numerous in England, which either have originally derived their name from, or have conferred it upon, some "local habitation."

In the present instance indeed the family before us evidently belongs to the former of these two classes, and has doubtless received its "unde derivatur" from a place; but seeing there are towns or villages called Bradford in no fewer than five English counties, to wit, Yorkshire, Somersetshire, Devonshire, Wiltshire, and Dorsetshire, we need not curiously inquire, at least it would be to no purpose if we did, which of the said counties, or the said towns in them, was the residence of the first Bradford of Bradford, the town or village itself having in times long before received its own designation from the broad ford which gave a passage to the "rude forefathers of the hamlet" over the river or stream on the banks of which they had pitched their tent.

The family of Bradford derives from an ancient house, and has the honour of numbering among its ancestors the ever-memorable and noble BRADFORD the MARTYR.

CHATSWORTH,

NEAR BAKEWELL, DERBYSHIRE.—DUKE OF DEVONSHIRE.

THE situation of Chatsworth is exceedingly beautiful, in the romantic part of Derbyshire which Sir Walter Scott has celebrated in "Peveril of the Peak."

The house stands in a park upwards of eleven miles in circumference, stocked with immense herds of deer, and diversified with every variety of scenery—the heather-covered hill and sheltered valley, wooded height and gentle slope, the whole studded with majestic trees, the growth of centuries.

Chetelsworthe would seem to have been the original name of the place; derived from a Saxon owner named Chetel, the other part of the word meaning "Court."

In Domesday Book the word is written Chetesworth, and at the time of the Norman survey the manor belonged to the Crown, and was in the keeping of William Peveril.

It afterward, for many years, was held by a family named Leech.

It was sold by them to the Agards.

It was purchased from them by Sir William Cavendish, ancestor of the Dukes of Devonshire, the owners since.

The old manor house was pulled down by him; but he only lived to begin the new mansion, dying in 1557. His widow, however, Elizabeth, the famous "Bess of Hardwick," continued and completed the work.

During the civil wars Chatsworth was occupied at times by both parties. In 1643 it was garrisoned by Sir John Gell for the Parliament, but was recovered for the King the same year by the Earl of Newcastle, who placed a garrison in it under Colonel Eyre. In 1645 it was again held for the King by Colonel Shallcross, of Shallcross Hall, and was besieged by four hundred Parliamentarians under Colonel Gell, but he was forced to return after fourteen days attack.

Mary Queen of Scots was confined here during part of the years 1570, 1573, 1577, 1578, and 1581, and a small raised tower near the bridge still preserves the name of the Bower.

It is approached by a bridge over the river between Chatsworth and the village of Edensor, a veritable model village. The bridge was built by Paine, supposed to be from a design by Michael Angelo, and ornamented with fine marble figures by Cibber.

The house is ornamented inside with paintings, chiefly by Verrio, Laguerre, Ricard, Huyd, Highmore, and Sir James Thornhill, and wood carving by Gibbons, Watson, Young, Lobb, and Davis; and on the outside with stone carving by Cibber, Gecraerslius, Watson, Harris, Nost, Nedauld, Davis, Landscroom, and Auriol.

Along the whole of the front, extending upwards of one thousand two hundred feet, is the ornamental flower garden of singular beauty.

The following particulars are derived from The Guide Book.

The Hall contains numerous antique busts and figures, and two splendid vases which occupy the side openings of the North Corridor. This corridor has a tesselated pavement, tastefully inlaid with a variety of beautiful marbles, and is otherwise ornamented. Along the side walls are arranged some fine antiques, supported on brackets.

The Great Hall is sixty feet by twenty-seven feet. The mosaic floor was laid by Watson. The decorations by Verrio and Laguerre, are taken from the history of Julius Cæsar. In one compartment is represented the crossing of the Rubicon; in another his voyage across the Adriatic to his army at Brundusium; the left side contains his sacrifice previous to going to the Senate, after the closing of the temple of Janus; over the north entrance is his Death; and on the ceiling his Deification: the whole is wonderfully executed.

The Great South Staircase is adorned with paintings, and figures occupy the niches.

The State Apartments form the most magnificent portion of the oldest part of the mansion:—the ceilings exhibit the productions of the pencils of Verrio and Sir James Thornhill, among which are the Judgment of Paris,—Phæton taking charge of the horses of the Sun,—Aurora, as the Morning Star, chasing away Night,—the Discovery of Mars and Venus,—and other mythological subjects. The floors are of oak, curiously inlaid, and the whole suite lined with wood of the choicest description, and furnished with costly cabinets, paintings by the old masters, and Gobelin tapestries of the Cartoons of Raphael.

In these rooms will be found many very rare and curious productions of art, ancient and modern: they contain the principal portion of the carvings in wood, so justly celebrated, and which have been noticed by Horace Walpole as the work of Gibbons. They comprise representations of dead game, fish, flowers, etc., grouped in a most admirable manner,—grouse, pheasants, partridges, quail, snipe, and woodcocks; the flowers exhibit the buoyancy and freshness of life.

The State Bed-room contains a bed of George II.; and also the chairs and footstools used at the coronation of George III. and Queen Charlotte. The fine canopy wrought by the Countess of Shrewsbury, and the wardrobe of Louis XIV. are also here.

In the State Music Room are the two gorgeously gilt chairs in which William IV. and Queen Adelaide were crowned. Here is a fine portrait of the first Duke of Devonshire in his robes of State by Mytems or Paul Vansomer.

In the State Drawing Room is a striking bust of Louis XIV., the head of which is bronze, and the lower portion of oriental alabaster. Here is also a model of a Russian Farm.

In the State Dining Room are busts on brackets:—William, fifth Duke of Devonshire; Francis, Duke of Bedford; Charles James Fox; and Lord George and Lady Cavendish. On a table of polished malachite (a present from Alexander I. of Russia,) stands the elegant malachite clock presented to His Grace by the late Czar Nicholas, accompanied by two fine square vases of the same material. Numerous other embellishments enhance the beauty of these magnificent rooms. The length of the suite is about one hundred and ninety feet. The view from these apartments is extremely beautiful. Overlooking the ornamental and extensive pleasure-grounds, enriched with every device of art, the eye wanders through the pleasant vale of Chatsworth to the wooded heights of Stanton and the green hill sides of Darley Dale.

The South Galleries.—In the upper of these Galleries are upwards of a thousand original drawings of a deeply interesting character, by Rubens, Salvator Rosa, Claude Lorraine, Raphael, Titian, Correggio, and others.

The Red Velvet Room (Billiard Room) abounds in beautiful pictures and art treasures. Its ceiling is richly decorated by Sir James Thornhill. Here is Eastlake's splendid picture of the Spartan Isidas. Here too is Bolton Abbey in the Olden Time, by Landseer.

The Great Drawing Room is a noble apartment, richly furnished and stored with valuable works of art. In this room is a table deserving particular attention; it is composed of different splendid minerals of various colours, and is not surpassed in beauty by anything of the kind in the house.

The Library is the second of the long range of rooms forming the east front, an extent of nearly five hundred and sixty feet. Count Bjornstjerne, the Swedish Ambassador, on seeing this suite of rooms opened, pronounced it to be the finest in Europe.

The Great Library is one of the most splendid rooms in Chatsworth, and finished in a style unique in richness, elegance, and beauty. The ground of the ceiling is white, adorned with burnished gold ornamental work in basso relievo, forming a splendid framework to five circular paintings set like precious gems within. The bookcases are of Spanish mahogany, and are divided into compartments by semi-circular metallic columns, richly gilt; these expand into a finely formed leaf, and support the floor of a gallery carried along three sides of the room, for the convenience of reaching books from the upper shelves. The gallery, which is approached by a secret stair, is defended by a handsome carved balustrade, ornamented with dead and burnished gold. The chimney-piece is of Carrara marble, finely sculptured in columns of wreathed foliage, and surmounted by a magnificent mirror, six feet by four feet six inches.

The Ante-Library is fitted up in the same style. The ceiling is adorned with a beautiful picture by Hayter, and two smaller subjects by Charles Landseer. An immense collection of medallions of distinguished persons, ancient and modern, are among the curiosities of this room. A door on the west side opens into the Great North Staircase, which is distinguished for its beauty and extent; it is of oak, with richly carved balustrades, and contains portraits of the late Emperor of Russia and his Consort; Richard, third Earl of Burlington; and George IV. in his robes, by Sir Thomas Lawrence.

The Cabinet Library has a splendid coved ceiling, divided into compartments, and supported by columns of beautiful marble, rising from pedestals of pure statuary, and surmounted with richly gilt Corinthian capitals.

The Dining Room is the most splendid apartment in Chatsworth. The ceiling is slightly coved, and divided into numerous gilt panels on a ground of the purest white. The deep plinth that surrounds the room, and all below the sur-base, are of polished Hopton marble. The walls are adorned with family portraits, by Vandyke, Honthorst, and Sir Godfrey Kneller. The door-cases are columns of Sicilian jasper and African marble, based on suitable pedestals, and surmounted with Ionic capitals. The two chimney-pieces are unique in design, tastefully sculptured in the purest statuary, and adorned with life-sized figures in full relief: one is by the younger Westmacott, the other by Siever.

The Ante-room contains two figures, in statuary marble; very appropriate ornaments for the positions they occupy, on each side the entrance to

The Sculpture Gallery.—This splendid saloon is one hundred and three feet in length; it is the depository of the finest works of art in Chatsworth.

The Orangery is a noble room, one hundred and eight feet long, well stored with orange trees of fine growth, some of which formed part of the collection of the Empress Josephine, at Malmaison; a Rhododendron Arboreum from Nepaul; choice exotics, and an infinite variety of shrubs and flowers.

The Gardens are very extensive, ranging from the house southward and eastward; and tastefully laid out in lawns and shrubberies, beautifully diversified with fountains and cascades. They abound in romantic scenes, serpentine walks, ornamented with sculptured figures and vases, picturesque trees, etc.

The Camellia House is well stocked with a variety of plants, which when blooming make a splendid show. The ground in front is laid out after the eastern style, with borders and shrubs interspersed with busts and figures, (among which are a colossal Flora, and two antiques, Isis and Orisis, brought by Mr. Banks from the great temple at Carnac,) and Chinese scent jars, which give the whole a beautiful appearance.

The Water Works (by Grillet,) are in the style of those at Versailles. The Great Cascade is situated on the side of the hill eastward of Chatsworth; the structure at its head resembles a temple, and is a good architectural object from different parts of the grounds. This building is ornamented with the carved heads of lions, dolphins, sea nymphs, etc., through which, when in play, as well as from the floors and sides, the water rushes in great force.

A road winds through the rocky defiles of the cliff. On the right is seen an immense rocking-stone, near to which is the entrance to the fountain known as the "Weeping Willow."

When the whole of the Water Works are in operation the scene is magnificent. The jets appear through and over the trees, and the dense water, rising in light wreathy columns, and reflected in the sun, contrasts beautifully with the varied foliage of the trees, and produces a most brilliant effect.

The Great Conservatory, before the erection of the Crystal Palace in 1851, was the most magnificent of its kind. The longest side is two hundred and seventy-six feet, and the shortest one hundred and twenty-three feet. It has a central arched roof sixty-seven feet high, with a span of seventy feet, resting on two rows of elegant iron pillars twenty-eight feet high, which divide the space about equally. The spaces between the ribs are filled in with light glazed framework, containing upwards of seventy thousand square feet of glass.   25 MH67

GUY'S CLIFFE,

THIS seat derives it double name from a person and a place, the former that of the redoubtable and famous "Guy, Earl of Warwick," the latter a high cliff which here bounds the western side of the classic Avon.

The story of Guy is thus told by my friend Sir Bernard Burke:—"Guy, who, like most of his brethren in the trade of knight-errantry, had much to answer for, bethinks himself at last that it is time to repent and amend, for which purpose, according to the most approved fashion of his day, he sets out upon a tedious pilgrimage. On his return to Britain he finds the country being harassed by Danish invaders, so that there was scarce a town or castle that they had not burnt or destroyed almost as far as Winchester. In the midst of their success these ferocious invaders proposed to King Athelstan three things,—either that he should resign his crown to the Danish generals; or should hold the realm of them; or that the dispute should be ended in a single combat by a champion of either side; when, if the Dane was beaten, his countrymen would free England of their presence; but if he prevailed, then the country without more ado should be given up in sovereignty to the Danes. Athelstan accepted the last of these propositions, but not one of his court felt inclined to match himself with the formidable giant Colbrand, the elected champion of the Danes. At this crisis Guy appears in his palmer's weeds, and is, with some difficulty, persuaded by the King to undertake the combat. What it was that induced Athelstan to place his fate and that of his kingdom in that of a wayworn, unknown pilgrim, is not explained by the chronicler, but the romancer unties the knot by the usual expedient in such cases. Athelstan had a vision instructing him to trust his defence to the first pilgrim he should meet at the entrance of his palace. The day of battle arrives, when the two combatants meet in the valley of Chilticumbe. Guy appears in the customary armour of a knight, but his adversary, the giant Colbrand, comes to the field with weapons enough to supply a whole host; he was 'so weightily harnessed that his horse could scarce carry him, and before him a cart loaded with Danish axes, great clubs with knobs of iron, square bars of steel, lances, and iron hooks to pull his adversary to him.' At this sight, notwithstanding his valour, Guy began to quake, or, as the romancer emphatically exclaims, 'never he was'n so sore afeard sith then he was born.'

It would seem, however, as in the case of the renowned French marshal, that it was his body and not his soul which was afraid, for he fought his battle right gallantly under every disadvantage. His horse is killed, his skull cleft in two, and his sword broken, but he makes a prayer to the Virgin, and snatching up an axe cuts off the giant's arm, who, for all that, 'held out the combat till the evening of that day,' when he fainted from loss of blood, and Guy incontinently cut off his head."

At the dissolution of the monasteries Guy's Cliffe was bestowed by Henry the Eighth on Andrew Flammock, of Flammock.

In later times it was possessed by a family named Edwards, and next passed to

SAMUEL GREATHEAD, ESQ., who built a new residence, and his son greatly enlarged and improved the place.

After him

BERTIE BERTIE GREATHEAD, ESQ. left a daughter and heiress married to

THE HON. CHARLES BERTIE PERCY, who thus became the owner of Guy's Cliffe.

Dugdale thus describes the scenery around. "A place this is of so great delight in respect of the river gliding below the rock, the dry and wholesome situation, and the fair groves of lofty elms overshadowing it, that to one who desireth a retired life, either for his devotions or study, the like is not to be found." Leland also thus,—"It is a house of pleasure, place meet for the Muses; there is silence, a pretty wood, antra in vivo saxo, the river rouling over the stones with a pretty noyse, "nemusculum ibidem opacum, fontes liquidi et gemmei, prata florida, antra muscosa, rivi levis et per saxa discursus, necnon solitudo et quies Musis amicissima," that is, "a thick grove there, liquid and sparkling fountains, flowery meads, mossy caverns, the gentle flow of a river over rocks, and also solitude and quiet most friendly to the Muses."

Within the house is a splendid collection of paintings, many of them from the easel of a young artist, Mr. Greathead, a son of the then family. The talents of the youthful painter were of such high promise, that when he visited France during the short peace, instead of sharing the fate of the other *detenus*, he was allowed by the special grace of Napoleon to retire to Italy. There however, he unfortunately died of a fever, at the early age of twenty-three. In addition to his works, many paintings by the most eminent masters are to be seen here, such as Cuyp, Canaletti, Spagnoletto, Holbein, and others of no less celebrity.

———

The family of Percy, Earls of Beverley and Dukes of Northumberland, of the former of which is the present owner of Guy's Cliffe, descends from Sir Hugh Smithson, who married Lady Elizabeth Seymour, the heiress of the Percies, and was created Duke of Northumberland in 1776.

The House of Percy had derived from William de Percy, one of the Norman chieftains who accompanied WILLIAM the Conqueror in 1066, and deduced his name from the village of Percy, near Villedieu.

KNOWSLEY HALL,

NEAR PRESCOT, LANCASHIRE.—EARL OF DERBY.

THE family of the Stanleys, Earls of Derby, is second, says Sir Bernard Burke, to none in the Peerage of England; and the pages of history well attest the truth of the remark, on which the "last words of Marmion" have further set the seal of poetry.

Knowsley Hall is finely and conspicuously situated in the Hundred of West Derby, in the County of Lancaster, and thence, and not from the town of Derby, as might be supposed, the Earl of Derby derives his title. It has been altered, enlarged, reduced in size, and again rebuilt, by one or other of its various possessors in the course of centuries.

The estate was originally, as given in "Domesday Book," Chenulneslei, and was held at the time of the survey by the family of Uchtred, together with other manors. It next passed to the De Knowsleys, and from them to the Lathams, and then to the Stanleys, through the marriage of Sir Thomas Stanley, Lord Deputy of Ireland, with Isabel, daughter of Sir Thomas Latham, of Latham and Knowsley, in the reign of Richard the Second.

The house was greatly enlarged by the first Earl of Derby for his son-in-law, King Henry the Seventh, in whose service he had so greatly distinguished himself, and on whose head, as Earl of Richmond, he placed the crown on Bosworth Field on the death of Richard the Third. At the ensuing coronation he acted as Lord High Steward.

The principal part of the mansion was built by James, the tenth Earl, in the reigns of King William the Third, Queen Anne, and King George the Second.

The east front is occupied by a private chapel, and on the south is a corridor, over which are the arms of the family, with the following inscription:—"James, Earl of Derby, Lord of Man and the Isles, grandson of James, Earl of Derby, and of Charlotte, daughter of Claude, Duke de la Tremouille, whose husband James was beheaded at Bolton, 15th. October, 1652, for strenuously adhering to Charles the Second, who refused a bill passed unanimously by both Houses of Parliament, for restoring to the family the estates lost by his loyalty to him, 1732."

The park is the largest in the county, being between nine and ten miles in circumference. It is ornamented by plantations and trees of ancient growth, and graced in front by a lake nearly a mile in length. Beautiful views are obtained from the higher grounds, especially towards the sea.

The paintings are numerous and valuable, especially Belshazzar's Feast, by Rembrandt, and the suicide, if so it may be called, of Seneca in the bath by Rubens.

There is a curious collection of family portraits, twenty-two of which were etched by Hamlet Winstanley, a pupil of Sir Godfrey Kneller, and published under the title of the "Knowsley Gallery."

The apartments are very fine, and of large size.

The family of the Stanleys were Lords paramount of the Isle of Man and the Isles, from the reign of Henry the Fourth to that of George the Second, holding under the Crown by the service of presenting two Falcons to the King on his coronation day. It derives from Adam de Aldithley, who is stated to have come with Duke William at the conquest to England, and his grandson, William de Aldithley, marrying the only daughter and heiress of Thomas Stanley, of Stafford, and having received with her the manor of Thalk, in Staffordshire, exchanged it with his cousin, Adam de Aldithley, for Stanley, which he made his seat, and assumed the name of the place as his own, in honour of his wife, who was of noble Saxon descent.

GARNSTONE,

NEAR WEOBLEY, HEREFORDSHIRE.—PEPLOE.

———

THIS is another of those old seats which in process of time has frequently changed, by descent in the female line, the name of its owners, as thus—

BIRCH, of Birch, Lancashire, was father of

SAMUEL BIRCH, born about the year 1600, of Ardwick and Ordshall, in the same shire, who left a son,

JOHN BIRCH, born in the year 1626, who became of Garnstone, and was a Colonel in the Parliamentary Army, and also M.P. for Weobley. In the former capacity he took the city of Hereford in 1645, and ransacked the Bishop's Palace, lawlessness being the habit of the Cromwellers. His daughter,

SARAH BIRCH, heiress of Garnstone, married her cousin,

JOHN BIRCH, who left the property to his brother,

SAMUEL BIRCH, from whom it descended to his nephew,

JOHN PEPLOE, (son of Ann Birch and Samuel Peploe, Warden of Manchester,) who took the name of Birch, and the property thus passed to his son,

SAMUEL PEPLOE, who dropped the name of Birch, died in the year 1845, and was succeeded by his nephew,

DANIEL PEPLOE WEBB, who dying in 1866, the property was inherited by his brother,

THE REV. JOHN BIRCH WEBB, who then also took the name of PEPLOE.

The present house was commenced in the year 1805 by Samuel Peploe, Esq. It is in the castellated style, and of grey stone.

The old house stood higher up in the park.

There is a finely wooded deer park of about two hundred acres. It contains a number of ancient cedar trees and venerable Scotch firs.

The place is situated about a mile from the town of Weobley, an old borough which formerly returned two Members to Parliament, but is now disfranchised.

From one side of the house there is a fine view of the Clee Hills and the Welsh Mountains, and on the other side Robin Hood's Butts are to be seen.

The following epitaph on Colonel Birch is to be seen on his tomb in Weobley Church:—

In Hope of Resurrection to Eternal Life
Here is deposited the Body of
COLL. JOHN BIRCH,
(Descended of a Worthy family in Lancashire.)
As the dignities He arrived at in the Field; and the
Esteem Universally yielded him in the Senat-House
Exceeded the attainments of most; so they were but the
Moderate and just rewards of this
Courage, Conduct, Wisdom, and Fidelity.
None who knew him denyed him ye charatter of
Asserting and vindicating
Ye Laws and Liberties of his country in War
And of promoting its Welfare and Prosperity in Peace.
He was borne ye 7th. of Sept., 1626,
And died (a Member of ye Honble. House of Comons,
Being Burgess for Weobley)
May ye 10th., 1691.

Of the present family is Mrs. Webb, the well-known authoress.

TRENTHAM HALL,

———

THE silver Trent gives its name to this grand ducal residence, built as it is on the site of some house which in Saxon times stood upon its bank, and thence originated the word which now composes the second part of the title of the present mansion.

Trentham Hall is situated about four miles north-west of the town of Newcastle-under-Lyne, and about five in a nearly opposite direction from that of Stone.

The Trent winds through the park, and furnishes in perfection the feature without which no landscape is complete. In one part it is widened into a lake, of about eighty acres in extent. The higher hills above command beautiful and extensive views of the surrounding country.

The grounds in the immediate vicinity of the house were originally laid out by "Capability Brown," and possessing in themselves the greatest natural advantages, have since had every embellishment and improvement that taste and wealth could add.

The apartments within the house are magnificent and spacious, and their walls are adorned with an extensive collection of paintings by ancient and modern artists.

The Church, which is an elegant building, is situated close to the house.

The park contains about five hundred acres of land, and is stocked with a fine herd of deer.

The pleasure grounds and gardens consist of about sixty-five acres. In one part stands the hollow trunk of an ancient yew tree, but still bearing several branches with leaves, supposed to have been planted about twelve hundred years since.

Between the churchyard and the Hall there stood a Nunnery in former times, a portion of the wall of which still remains.

The estate of Trentham came into the possession of the family of the Duke of Sutherland through the marriage of Sir Thomas Gower with Frances, daughter and co-heiress of Sir John Leveson, Knight, of Lilleshall, Staffordshire, and Haling, in Kent, who bequeathed the whole of his extensive property to his nephew, Sir William Leveson Gower.

Trentham has had the honour of Royal visits from King George the Third in 1805, the Princess Victoria in 1832, and the Prince and Princess of Wales in 1866, and again in 1867.

The family of the Duke of Sutherland derives from Sir Allan Gower, Lord of Stittenham, in Yorkshire, at the time of the Conquest.

Upon the visit of George the Fourth to Scotland in 1822, it was determined by His Majesty that the right of carrying the sceptre before the King was vested in the Earls of Sutherland.

11 MA 67

CHARLECOTE.

CHARLECOTE,

NEAR STRATFORD-ON-AVON, WARWICKSHIRE.—LUCY.

———

NOT to know Charlecote "argues one's self unknown," for it is to confess to ignorance of "Justice Shallow," and therefore of Shakespeare himself.

> *Falstaff.* You have here a goodly house and a rich.
> *Shallow.* Barren, barren, barren; beggars all, beggars all, Sir John; marry good air!

The knight's opinion, rather than the disparaging one of the owner, will be that of every one who can appreciate the beauty of an old English mansion.

On the banks of the winding Avon, about four miles from the native place of the great poet, stands Charlecote Hall, the ancient seat of the Lucy family.

In Saxon times the castle was possessed by one of the name of

SAXI. It subsequently was held by the

EARL OF MELLENT, from whom it passed to his brother,

HENRY DE NEWBURGH, Earl of Warwick, who enfeoffed with it

THURSTANE DE MONTFORT, whose son,

HENRY DE MONTFORT, bestowed it on

WALTER, son of Thurstane de Charlecote, or Cherlcote, (a son probably of De Montfort,) who by his wife Cicely had a son

WILLIAM DE CHARLECOTE, who changed his name to

LUCY, in consequence, as is supposed by Sir William Dugdale, of his mother having been a Norman heiress of that name. He was one of the bold Barons who took up arms against King John, and was in consequence deprived of his lands, which were, however, subsequently restored to him in the first year of the reign of the succeeding monarch.

A long line of knightly descendants followed him, and in the Wars of the Roses the then head of the family took the side of the House of York, and his great grandson,

SIR THOMAS LUCY, of Charlecote, who lived under King Edward the Sixth and Queen Elizabeth, rebuilt the manor house, as it now stands in all its main features, in the first year of the reign of the latter. He was Member of Parliament for Warwickshire, and a Justice of the Peace—the "Justice Shallow" of the "Merry Wives of Windsor."

1.   K

After a further succession of heads of the family, this long-descended line ended in

GEORGE LUCY, ESQ., High Sheriff of Warwickshire in 1769, who died in 1786, when the "Historic Lands" of Charlecote passed to

THE REV JOHN HAMMOND, who assumed by sign manual, in 1787, the surname and arms of Lucy.

The family of the above Rev. John Hammond descended from the Rev. John Hammond and Alice his wife, daughter of Sir Fulke Lucy.

RIPLEY CASTLE

RIPLEY CASTLE,

NEAR KNARESBOROUGH, YORKSHIRE.—INGILBY, BARONET.

IF there is a "model village" anywhere in England, I think it is Ripley, and the richness and beauty of the country around make a fitting frame in which the picture is set.

Ripley Castle is the ancient seat of the baronetical family of Ingilby. It stands on land not far from the river Nidd, the name denoting a pasture on the bank of a stream.

The house is a castellated building, and was erected in the year 1555, as appears from the following inscription carved in the frieze of the wainscot in one of the chambers of the tower:—

In the yeire of our Ld. MDLV.,
was this house buylded
by Sir William Ingilby, Knight,
Philip and Marie reigning that time.

It has, however, been much altered and enlarged in the years that have since passed, and the greenhouses and hothouses are said to be scarcely exceeded by any in the kingdom.

On a stained glass window in the principal staircase are exhibited the quarterings and intermarriages of the Ingilby family, during a period of four hundred and forty three years.

At the entrance of the village on the north side is a school-house, built in the year 1702, over the door of which is the inscription:—

This school was built by Mary Ingilby,
in the year 1702;
and endowed with part of the fortune of
Catherine Ingilby;
being the two youngest daughters of
Sir William Ingilby, of Ripley,
in the county of York, Baronet.

"After the battle of Marston Moor, Cromwell took the route to Ripley, and sent to the castle by an officer, a relation to the Ingilbys, to announce his arrival in that town. Sir William was at that time from home, but his lady, the daughter of Sir James Bellingham, who received the communication, requested that Cromwell might be told, that no such person as himself could be admitted there, adding that she had force enough to defend herself and that house against all rebels. With some persuasion, this heroic lady was at length prevailed upon by her relative to receive the General, which she did at the gate of the lodge, with a pair of pistols stuck in her apron strings; and having told him that she expected that neither he nor his soldiers would behave improperly, she led him to the hall. There sitting or reclining, each on a sofa, in different parts of the room, these two extraordinary personages passed the night, equally jealous of each others' intentions. At his departure in the morning, this high-spirited dame caused it to be intimated to Cromwell, that it was well he had behaved in so peaceable a manner, for had it been otherwise, he would not have left that house alive."

Sir Thomas de Ingilby, about the year 1378, married the heiress of the Ripley family, and with her acquired the estate.

The Baronetcy was conferred on the then possessor in the year 1642, who accordingly became

SIR WILLIAM INGILBY.

The fourth Baronet,

SIR JOHN INGILBY, died unmarried in the year 1772, when the Baronetcy became extinct; but it was subsequently revived in 1781, in his successor,

SIR JOHN INGILBY. It afterwards became extinct again, and has recently been revived in the person of the

REV. HENRY INGILBY, of Ripley Castle, who has been created a Baronet.

The family of Ingilby deduces from Sir Thomas Ingleby, or de Ingilby, as above stated.

BURGHLEY HOUSE

BURGHLEY HOUSE,

NEAR STAMFORD, LINCOLNSHIRE.—MARQUIS OF EXETER.

BURGHLEY, or Burleigh House, was begun and mostly built in the reign of Elizabeth by the celebrated

WILLIAM CECIL, LORD BURLEIGH.

In one of his letters, dated 1585, he says, "My house of Burleigh is of my mother's inheritance, who liveth, and is the owner thereof, and I but a farmer; and for the building there, I have set my walls on the old foundations. Indeed, I have made the rough stone walls to be square, and yet one side remaineth as my father left it me."

Over one of the entrances within a central court, is the following inscription recording an earlier period of the work:—"W. Dom. De Burghley 1577." Beneath the turret is the date of 1585, when many great additions were made to the building. The grand entrance towards the north appears to have been added in the year 1587. Since these dates many other additions and alterations have been made, the whole of the house surrounding a central court.

To the south is a fine sloping lawn, with a broad sheet of water, and views of park scenery. On the west side are similar home views, and distant ones of objects in Rutlandshire, Lincolnshire, and the spires of Stamford. On the north side the ground slopes to the river Welland, and an extensive tract of country is in sight.

About two miles to the west of Burghley House are the ruins of Wothorp, or Worthorp House, where, according to Camden, a mansion of considerable size was built by Thomas Cecil, the then Earl of Burghley, who is recorded to have said that "he built it only to retire to out of the dust, while his great house at Burghley was sweeping." The Duke of Buckingham resided here for some years after the Restoration.

In the dining-room is a large silver fountain, and two oval silver cisterns adorned with lions, the supporters of the family arms, the weight of the smaller six hundred ounces, or forty-one pounds, and that of the larger three thousand ounces, or one hundred weight, three quarters, nine pounds, supposed to be the largest piece of plate in Europe.

In the jewel closet is a golden basin and spoon, said to have been used at the coronation of Queen Elizabeth.

There is a brilliant collection of pictures in the house.

———

The family of the Marquis of Exeter descends from Robert Cyssel, or Cecil, an officer of the court, and in attendance on Henry the Eighth at the celebrated meeting between that monarch and Francis, King of France, on the "Field of the Cloth of Gold."

ALTON TOWERS,

NEAR CHEADLE, STAFFORDSHIRE.—EARL OF SHREWSBURY AND TALBOT.

THE princely seat of Alton Towers, sometimes called Alton Abbey, the name itself of Alton being a contraction of Alveton, is situated in the hundred of Totmonslow, near the town of Stafford.

A Castle was erected here soon after the Norman Conquest.

In the reign of King John it was possessed by

THEOBALD DE VERDON, whose daughter,

JOAN DE VERDON, carried it by marriage to

THOMAS LORD FURNIVAL.

In process of time the heiress of the family,

MAUD FURNIVAL, brought it into the present line by her marriage with

SIR JOHN TALBOT, afterwards created Earl of Shrewsbury, who had been victorious in no less than forty several battles and dangerous skirmishes, and was at last killed by a cannon in action—"The ruling passion strong in death"—at Chastillon sur Dordon, in 1453. "The great Alcides of the field, valiant Lord Talbot, Earl of Shrewsbury, created, for his rare success in arms, Great Earl of Washford, Waterford, and Valence, Lord Talbot of Goodrig and Urchinfield, Lord Strange of Blackmere, Lord Verdon of Alton, Lord Cromwell of Wingfield, Lord Furnival of Sheffield;"

> "The thrice victorious Lord of Falconbridge,
> Knight of the noble order of Saint George,
> Worthy Saint Michael and the Golden Fleece,
> Great Mareshal to Henry the Sixth,
> Of all his wars within the realm of France."

During the Cromwellian usurpation, the ancient castle, which was built on a precipitous rock, below which flowed the river Churnet, was destroyed by his ignorant soldiery.

The present magnificent mansion is of an irregular form, with gables and embattled towers, whence its name.

The drive through the park leads by a lodge, at the foot of a steep hill, from the town of Alton, and for more than a mile lies through pine woods.

The drawing-room opens into a fine conservatory.

The garden and pleasure-grounds are extremely beautiful and picturesque.

In one part is placed a statuary head of Pitt, and opposite to it is another conservatory.

The noble family of Talbot derives its origin from Saxon times; but its first recorded ancestor is Robert de Talbot, whose name is given in Domesday Book, as holding nine hides of land from Walter Giffard, Earl of Buckingham.

11 MA 67

BROADLANDS.

BROADLANDS,

NEAR ROMSEY, HAMPSHIRE.—LORD PALMERSTON.

———

THOUGH I have been in the immediate neighbourhood of this well-known seat myself—well known from the name of its late owner, whose title for half a century has been "familiar in our ears as a household word,"—I shall let Sir Bernard Burke describe the scenery around it, for no one could do it better, no writer that I know can do it so well.

"Few seats are surrounded by a fairer landscape than this of Broadlands. The park, of an irregular shape, extends about a mile and a quarter to the River Test, which here unites its various branches into a single channel, and spreads out into a broad expanse of ornamental water. This park exhibits many noble trees of various kinds, scattered singly, or in groups, arranged with exquisite taste and effect. On the side that abuts on Romsey it is about half a mile in length.

The width of the valley of the Test is here almost three quarters of a mile, if measured from the commencement of the rise on either side. Above Romsey it extends westward into a sort of basin, and again widens in the same direction opposite the middle of the entire length of Broadlands. Between these points it is narrowed by hills that jut out in gentle swellings, one of which slopes, lawn-like, towards the meadows, while the other stands out like a fortress made by nature, and indeed bears the marks of having been once artificially fortified upon all except its steepest sides. The summit is remarkably flat, and covered with a green turf as soft to the tread as velvet. Mingled with the grass is an abundance of wild thyme and other aromatic herbage, so that on a fine summer's day the whole place glitters with the glance of tiny wings, and the air is alive with the busy hum of bees, attracted thither by the fragrance.

From the top of this eminence the views are exceedingly beautiful; and their effect is not a little heightened by their being broken and separated by clumps of trees, that are variously dispersed upon the crown and margin of the hill. These views are principally four, though of course they may yet be diversified if the spectators take up other positions. First, upon the right hand is a prospect down the valley, and across Southampton water to the New Forest: perhaps it may even extend, as the peasants of the neighbourhood say it does, to the Isle of Wight; but for this the day must be fine, and the atmosphere remarkably free from vapour; it may be doubted, too, whether much would be gained to the spectator by this extension of his prospect, for nothing can be well imagined more beautiful than the nearer landscape, when the clouds, under the influence of a gentle west wind, are flinging their light shadows upon it, and for a moment interrupting the sunshine. Secondly, to the left of the scene just mentioned, is the view of Broadlands, forming with its home park a graceful contrast to the beauties of nature. Thirdly, comes the view of Romsey, the only objection to which is the too great remoteness of the abbey church, the most interesting feature that the town presents. Lastly, there is the view up the valley of the Test, which here assumes the appearance of an amphitheatre with finely-wooded margins, the bright streams glittering among fields of the freshest verdure; while here and there some blighted trunk of a tree stands out amongst all this life and youth like a churchyard in some crowded city, as if to remind us that the scene, after all, is fleeting."

Among the principal paintings here are,—a large landscape by Salvator Rosa, a second and third by Nicholas Poussin, a fourth by Swanaret, a fifth by Eugydare, a sixth by Claude Lorraine, and a seventh by Wouvermann, with men and horses, the *forte* of that great painter, far exceeded, however, by our own Landseer. Also a "Young Man's Head," by Carraci; the "Head of an Old Man," by Rembrandt; the "Descent from the Cross," by Domenichino, (this last a copy from Dan da Volterro.) There is also a fine collection of statuary, and in particular a head of Juno.

The family of Lord Palmerston derived, as is believed, from Algar, Earl of Mercia, living about the year 1000.

TEMPLE NEWSAM.

TEMPLE NEWSAM,

NEAR LEEDS, YORKSHIRE.—MEYNELL-INGRAM.

———

EVERY one that has read "Ivanhoe,"—as who that ever has been young has not?—every one that knows it by heart,—as who does not?—will recall at the name of this seat the vivid and stirring descriptions therein given us of those Warrior-monks, the Knights Templars, who once, as Sir Bernard Burke writes in his account of this place, set their mailed feet upon the neck of Kings, and had well-nigh been an over-match for the Pope himself.

Here, in those distant times, was a Preceptory of this order of Military Churchmen, and one cannot but at once summon up before the eye of the mind their Grand Master, Lucas de Beaumanoir, at the head of his knightly followers, Maurice de Bracy, fresh from the fray at Coningsburgh Castle and the ruined towers of Torquilstone, Waldemar Fitzurse, Brian de Bois Guilbert, Conrade de Montfichet, and Albert Malvoisin, and "see them on their winding way," as with their troop of 'free lances" they slowly move off from Templestowe, in "long and glittering line," to the music of a wild march from some distant Eastern land, and follow the waving banner of Beau-seant. When, however, and none too soon, they were suppressed by the hand of a stronger power, the estate was granted by King Edward the Third to

SIR JOHN DARCY, with whose descendants it remained until

THOMAS, LORD DARCY, got into trouble with "Bluff Hall," who was not the man to brook opposition at the hand of a subject, and, on suspicion of his having delivered up Pontefract Castle to the Yorkshiremen in the "Pilgrimage of Grace," forthwith made an end of him on Tower Hill. It is, however, considered by historians far from certain that the unfortunate nobleman was really guilty of complicity in the rebellion.

The king thereupon bestowed the estate on

MATTHEW, EARL OF LENNOX, whose son,

LORD DARNLEY, husband of the Queen of Scots, was born here. It was next granted by King James the First to the then

DUKE OF LENNOX, by whom it was sold to

SIR ANTHONY INGRAM, who built the present splendid mansion upon it. His descendant,

LORD IRVINE, left with other daughters,

ELIZABETH IRVINE (SHEPHERD,) who married, 2nd. of August, 1782,

HUGO MEYNELL, ESQ., of Hoar Cross in the county of Stafford, and so brought it and the additional surname of Ingram into the present family.

Temple Newsam stands upon the bank of the River Aire, about four miles from Leeds and fourteen from York, in a part of the country which is naturally very beautiful, as indeed are most parts of the Yorkshire manufacturing districts, but much marred, for the present, that is to say until our coal fields are exhausted, by the smoke that arises from so many furnaces.

———

The family of Meynell-Ingram derives through a long line from Gilbert de Mesnil, living in the reign of Henry the Second, supposed to be descended from Hugh de Grent-Mesnil, a potent Norman Baron.

WOLLATON HALL

WOLLATON HALL,

NEAR NOTTINGHAM, NOTTINGHAMSHIRE.—LORD MIDDLETON.

WOLLATON HALL, a stately structure, is situated on a knoll near the River Trent, between two and three miles from Nottingham, and is approached by an avenue of noble lime trees nearly a mile in length.

It stands in an extensive park, amply wooded with ancient oaks and elms, and well stocked with deer, the ground undulated and adorned with sheets of water.

The house was built by Sir Francis Willoughby, who commenced the work in the year 1580 and completed it in 1588.

The library contains a valuable collection of books, as also the ancient Service Book of Wollaton Church, and portraits of Willughby the eminent naturalist, Ray his contemporary, and the sixth Lord Middleton.

In the hall are several fine pictures, and among them one of the famous navigator Hugh Willoughby, who was sent out on a voyage in the reign of King Edward the Sixth, with three ships, to discover the famous and fabulous Cathay. He set sail in the year 1553, and having spent some time in cruising in the northern regions, was forced about the middle of September to put in to a harbour of Lapland, where he and the whole of his crew were frozen to death.

The gallery also contains some family portraits.

The Rev. Prebendary Trollope thus writes of it:—"Great is the fame of this mansion as a specimen of English domestic architecture, and but few, if any, will hesitate to acknowledge the justice of its high reputation. Here there is much for all to admire, but perhaps still more for lovers of architecture to study. Externally, this fine old fabric consists of two entirely distinctive portions, namely, the great dominant central tower and the remainder of the composition. These, although built at the same time, or nearly so, 1580-8, differ entirely from each other in proportion, style, and ornamentation."

"There is much dignified beauty about the principal front, with its double flight of balustraded steps leading to the door, for which the stately avenue leading to it has prepared the visitor; while the bold breaks of its *façade* ensure the valuable assistance of a sufficient amount of light and shade, which plays over its surface in varied masses when a sunny day smiles upon it, and its angle towers springing aloft, with their fretted gables and their obelisk pinnacles, lightly break the sky line in a charming manner. The garden front is of the same character, but instead of rising from a deer park, it has a stately terrace spread out before it, relieved by groups of fine evergreens and the lovely turf of an English lawn."

———

The family of Lord Middleton descends from Sir Christopher Willoughby, K.B., living in the reign of King Henry the Seventh.

INVERARY CASTLE.

INVERARY CASTLE,

NEAR INVERARY, ARGYLLSHIRE.—DUKE OF ARGYLL.

It is nothing new to say that most of the persons who travel to foreign lands, "in search of the sublime," have left still more beautiful scenery in their native land than much they see abroad, and are utterly ignorant of the mountains, valleys, hills, woodlands, plains, lakes, streams; and rivers, which adorn each of the three kingdoms of the British Islands. It is the old story over again of the substance being left for the shadow in many such cases. Inverary Castle offers a notable instance of this, standing in a situation of extreme beauty and grandeur, in the midst of a wide open space, surrounded by lofty hills which are covered with wood, and having in front Lough Fyne, a deep amphitheatre of water, indented on all sides of its shores with a succession and variety of promontories.

Immediately behind the house the hill of Dunicoick rises almost perpendicularly to the height of seven hundred and fifty feet, nearly covered with wood, through which are seen the projecting rocks of its native foundation and formation. It needs hardly to be added that the wide and extensive view from its summit is one of surpassing beauty, nature supplying in such abundance the materials to which art has added all that art can add. The plantations which adorn and diversify the scenery were begun by the then Marquis of Argyll in the reign of Charles the First, and his plans have been continued by his descendants ever since. The late Duke is stated to have devoted £3,000 a year to the improvement of the seat, feeling, as each successive proprietor of an estate should feel, that he is but a steward for those who come after him, and that thus he can best also benefit the present race of tenantry, who all have their own natural claims upon him as well.

The Park is extensive, graced with trees of ancient growth, and watered by the River Aray, a rapid stream, crossed by a bridge in one part, and afterwards falling into the above-named lake or arm of the sea.

The entrance hall is fitted up as an armoury, with a collection of the various weapons in use, or rather that were formerly in use, by the Highlanders,—

"An old hall hung about with pikes, guns, and bows,
With old swords, and bucklers that had borne many shrewde blows."

Above it is a gallery in which an organ is placed.

The great drawing-room is a splendid apartment, hung with tapestry, and ornamented in a most superb manner.

The turrets of the building are fitted up as small libraries or private rooms.

Mary Queen of Scots paid a visit to Inverary Castle in 1563.

The erection of the present castellated mansion was commenced in the memorable "'45," a time not favourable for building or the quiet arts of peace, and its completion was thus retarded for a time. The old building was taken down in the year 1770.

The portraits, as may be supposed, are numerous and interesting, among them being one of the unfortunate Marquis of Argyll who was beheaded May 27th., 1661. Also his son Archibald, the ninth Marquis, who was beheaded at the Cross of Edinburgh, June 30th., 1685. Others of a late Duke of Argyll, by Gainsborough; Lord Frederick Campbell, by Gainsborough; Douglas, sixth Duke of Hamilton, by Battoni; several landscapes representing views in the neighbourhood, by Nasmyth and Williams; some fine drawings by De Croc, and a numerous collection of prints by the best masters.

The family of the Duke of Argyll derives from Gillespick Campbell, living in the beginning of the thirteenth century.

16 AU 67

NEWSTEAD ABBEY,

NEAR MANSFIELD, NOTTINGHAMSHIRE.—WEBB.

———

NEWSTEAD ABBEY, "one of the finest specimens in existence of those quaint and romantic piles, half castle, half ornament, which remain as monuments of the olden times of England," is situated about five miles from Mansfield and nine miles north of Nottingham. It was originally a Friary of Black Canons, founded by Henry the Second in the year 1170. At the dissolution of the monasteries it was granted to Sir John Byron, Lieutenant of Sherwood Forest. It was besieged by the parliamentary forces, and after the murder of King Charles the First was confiscated by the Puritans, but was restored by Charles the Second to Lord Byron, who, in reward of his loyalty to the throne had been raised to the Peerage by Charles the First. It continued in the family till the year 1815, when it was sold to

COLONEL WILDMAN, and afterwards to

F. W. WEBB, ESQ.

Outside the building the principal objects worth seeing are a noble oak tree, a relique of the ancient forest; the upper lake, formed by keeping up the waters of the river Leen; the lower lake; and an aviary.

Inside are the entrance-hall; the monks' parlour, or reception room; the haunted chamber; the eastern corridor; the tapestry bedroom; the tapestry dressing-room; King Edward the Third's bedroom; King Henry the First's lodgings; the Duke of Sussex's sitting-room; the grand dining-hall; the breakfast-room; the cloisters; and the chapel.

In the following lines written by Lord Byron, he had Newstead in view; but the verses, *me judice*, are unworthy of the subject, an instance, *unum e multis*, by way of proof, how much a poet may be over-rated in his lifetime, to find his level in the deserved neglect of his writings in the next generation.

"Before the mansion lay a lucid lake,
 Broad as transparent, deep, and freshly fed
By a river, which its soften'd way did take
 In currents through the calmer water spread
Around: the wildfowl nestled in the brake
 And sedges, brooding in their liquid bed:
The woods sloped downwards to its brink, and stood
With their green faces fixed upon the flood."

I.   M

"Amidst the court a Gothic fountain play'd,
    Symmetrical, but deck'd with carvings quaint—
Strange faces, like to men in masquerade,
    And here perhaps a monster, there a saint:
The spring gush'd through grim mouths of granite made,
    And sparkled into basins, where it spent
Its little torrent in a thousand bubbles—
Like man's vain glory, and his vainer troubles."

The owner of Newstead Abbey is the son of Frederick Webb, Esq.

BLENHEIM,

NEAR WOODSTOCK, OXFORDSHIRE.—DUKE OF MARLBOROUGH.

"IF nothing were to be seen in England but this seat, with its park and treasures of art," writes Dr. Waagen, the Director of the Royal Gallery at Berlin, "there would be no reason to repent the journey to this country. The whole is on so grand a scale, that no prince in the world would need to be ashamed of it; and at the same time it is a noble monument of the gratitude of the English nation to the great Duke of Marlborough."

In the year 866 King Ethelred held a Parliament in Woodstock Palace. His successor, in 872,

ALFRED THE GREAT, occasionally resided there when not engaged in war, and is stated in a MS. in the Cottonian Library to have found leisure to translate "Boethius de Consolatione," and about the same time to have founded or restored the University of Oxford.

King Henry the First repaired or rebuilt the palace, and built a wall round the park.

Henry the Second received here the homage of Malcolm King of Scotland, and Rees Prince of Wales, in 1164.

Edward the First called a Parliament at this place in 1275; and here his second son, Edward, was born, thence named Edward of Woodstock.

EDWARD, eldest son of Edward the Third, commonly called the Black Prince, was also born here, as likewise Thomas, his sixth son.

Blenheim Palace was built by Sir John Vanbrugh, the architect, at the public expense, in the reign of Queen Anne, half a million of money being voted for its completion; and was conferred, together with the Honour of Woodstock, on John Duke of Marlborough, as a memorial of the royal favour and the gratitude of the public, for the very great victories he had gained over the French and Bavarians, particularly that near the village of Blenheim on the 2nd. of August, 1704. On the anniversary of the day every year a standard with the *fleurs-de-lys* painted on it is rendered at Windsor Castle as a quittance for all rents, suits, and services due to the crown, and in consequence a long series of flags is there exhibited.

The apartments, which are too numerous to be particularized, are nobly proportioned, and the architectural grandeur of the various rooms is abundantly supported by the richness of the furniture and fittings, and the value and beauty of the works of art and *vertù* that adorn them. In the library, which contains one of the largest collections of books in the country, is a statue of Queen Anne, by Rysbrach, as also a bust of Alexander the Great, from Herculaneum. In the chapel is the monument by Rysbrach, of the great Duke of Marlborough, 1722. The house has also an observatory and a theatre.

In the park is a fine expanse of water, over which is a bridge of three arches, the central one, one hundred and one feet span, being larger than that of the Rialto at Venice. In the grounds are also a temple of Diana built by Sir William Chambers; a column one hundred and thirty feet high, with a colossal statue of the great Duke at the top, and a record of his principal achievements on the pedestal; a triumphal arch, and numerous pieces of statuary.

The paintings at Blenheim, almost national in their number and value, are specimens by:—Abbati; Albano; Balen; Bamboccio; Baroccio; Bellini; Bourgognone; Boudewyns; Brauer; Bril; Canaletto, four; Annibale Caracci, four; Ludovico Caracci, two; Castiglione; Claude, two; Coques; Correggio, three; Clostermans; Cortona; Cosway, three; Cuyp; Dance; Delen; Dolci, four; Ferg, two; Franck, three; Gainsborough; Giordano, five; Giorgione, two; Guido; Holbein, three; Honthorst; Hudson, five; Jordaens, two; Kettle; Kneller, eighteen; Lairesse; Lancret, two; Lely, four; Maltese, two; Maratti; Mignard; Mola; Bartolomé Estevan Murillo, two; Disciple of Murillo; Mytens, two; Neefs; Arnold Vander Neer; Arturus Vander Neer; Nogari, two; Ostade; Pater; Poussin, two; Raffaelle, three; Reinagle; Rembrandt, three; Reynolds, ten; Marco Ricci, nine; Sebastiano Ricci; Romney, two; Roos; Rothenaimer, four; Rubens, twenty-five; Ruysdael; Sanders, three; Savery; Schalcken; Slaughton, two; Smith, two; Sneyders, three; Solimene; Steen; Strozzi; Tempesta, two; David Teniers, (called the old); David Teniers, (called the young) three; Tillemans, four; Tintoretto, two; Titian, thirteen; Vandyke, sixteen; Alessandro Veronese; Paolo Cagliari Veronese, three; Leonardo da Vinci; Walker; Watteau; Weeninx; Wootton, two; Wouvermans, three; Wyck.

The family of the Duke of Marlborough derives from Sir Robert Spencer, of Wormleighton, in the county of Northumberland, raised to the peerage by the title of Baron Spencer of Wormleighton, and whose descendant, Charles, fifth Earl of Sunderland, to which dignity the third baron had been elevated, brought the dukedom of Marlborough into the family on the demise of his aunt Henrietta, created Duchess of Marlborough under a special Act of Parliament, his father, the third Earl, having married her next sister Lady Anne Churchill.

The following anecdote is recorded of the first Baron Spencer. In a debate in Parliament on the royal prerogative, in 1621, Thomas Howard, Earl of Arundel, remarked to him, "My Lord, when these things were doing, your ancestors were keeping sheep." "When my ancestors were keeping sheep," replied Spencer, "your lordship's ancestors were plotting treason."

The family of Churchill was stated by Dr. James Anderson, in his genealogical tables, to be derived from Gitto de Leon, a Frenchman, whose son Wandril was Lord of Courcil, the name afterwards being altered to Chirchil, and then to Churchill.

CRANBURY PARK,

NEAR WINCHESTER, HAMPSHIRE.—CHAMBERLAYNE.

———

FEW mansions, even in the south of Hampshire, where country seats abound, are more delightfully situated than Cranbury. The hill on which it stands is one of the highest in the county, and from the extensive and picturesque pleasure-grounds beautiful views are obtained of Southampton Water and the Isle of Wight to the south; to the east are uninterrupted views over almost the whole of the south-eastern portion of Hampshire; while to the north the eye overlooks the lovely vale of Hursley as far as the pretty little village of Farley Chamberlayne.

The park is extensive and beautifully wooded, the timber being remarkably fine.

Cranbury House is a large mansion, built of red brick, with stone facings. It is difficult to say exactly when it was originally built, but it is certain that it is of great antiquity, and from traces of artificial fishponds discovered in the park, it is conjectured that it was formerly a monastery.

Cranbury was once the name of an extensive district, and mention is made of it in Domesday Book.

It contains a valuable collection of paintings by Sir Joshua Reynolds, Vandervelde, Le Brun, Callcott, Richter, Collins, Westall, Copley Fielding, Thompson, etc.; and some fine pieces of sculpture by Nollekens and Chantrey, one of which, a Venus by the former, was valued by the Commissioners of the International Exhibition at £2,000.

The ceiling in the saloon is very famous, the painting being the work of that eminent architect, the late Sir Nathaniel Holland.

Amongst the other objects of interest may be mentioned a fine large organ of great antiquity lately restored by Willis, and an instrument called an "Apollonicon," or self-playing organ, made in the Black Forest, in Germany, and exhibited in Leicester Square till it was purchased by Mr. W. Chamberlayne, uncle of the present owner of Cranbury, for many years M.P. for Southampton.

Mr. T. Chamberlayne inherited with Cranbury extensive property on the banks of Southampton Water, on a portion of which are situated the well-known ruins of Netley Abbey. Of the ancestors of the Chamberlayne family not a few figured prominently in the history of their country, amongst whom may be mentioned William Chamberlayne, Lord of North Ryston, chamberlain to Henry the Second, who made prisoner Robert de Bellemont, Earl of Leicester, in 1174. Also Sir John

Chamberlayne, who distinguished himself in the martial reign of Edward the Third, and whose descendants settled at Sherborne Castle, in Oxfordshire, which has since passed into the possession of the Earls of Macclesfield: from them, through the Chamberlaynes of Wickham, Baronets, is descended the present owner of Cranbury. The baronetcy alluded to became extinct in 1776.

The family of Chamberlayne trace their descent from John de Tankerville, a Norman baron, who was made Chamberlain—or, as it was then spelt, "Chamberlayne" —to King Henry the First, and whose descendants assumed the name.

SCONE PALACE,

NEAR PERTH, PERTHSHIRE.—EARL OF MANSFIELD.

SCONE PALACE, it need hardly be here stated, was in ancient times a favourite residence of the kings of Scotland, and the celebrated stone on which they sat when crowned, was carried from Scone by Edward the First, and is now placed in the coronation chair in Westminster Abbey. This stone is stated by Sir James Ware to have been first brought to Ireland by the colony of the Inath de Danans, and thence removed to Scotland when Fergus, the first king of Scotland, who was descended from the blood royal of Ireland, was crowned on it.

The situation of this seat is extremely beautiful, the Tay flowing at the edge of the park in view of the windows, while on the opposite side is the rich scenery about Perth, and on the right the Grampian Hills bound the distant view.

The palace and the abbey were both dilapidated under Henry the Eighth, but the former was restored in the early part of the seventeenth century, and here King Charles the Second was crowned in the year 1651, ten years before the ceremony was again performed in Westminster. Here also the Pretender, the Chevalier St. George, was crowned in 1715.

In the year 1803 the old palace was removed by the then Earl of Mansfield, and in its stead he erected the present mansion, which was completed in 1806. It is two hundred and twenty feet long, and the sides are one hundred and thirty on the north and the south.

The rooms are very fine, and contain many curiosities and paintings, and among the latter portraits of King Charles the Martyr, by Vandyke; the Marquis of Montrose; Lord Mansfield, the great lawyer, by Sir Joshua Reynolds; also his successor, and the next Earl and Countess, by Sir Thomas Lawrence.

In the state bedroom is a bed presented by King George the Third to the then Earl. It is of crimson damask, with the full arms of Britain embroidered in gold at the head and the top. In an adjoining room is a bed in which Queen Mary slept, the hangings worked by herself while a prisoner in Lochleven Castle; in another one which her son, James the Sixth of Scotland and First of England, used. In these apartments there are several curious portraits of members of the Royal House of Stuart.

In the cloisters, between the gallery and the corridor, are full-length portraits of

George the Third and Queen Charlotte, by Ramsay, and some ancient coats-of-arms, carved in stone and built into the wall.

There are in all in Scone Palace one hundred and twenty-five rooms, and it is stated that of these ninety are bedrooms.

In the library is the woolsack on which the Lord Chief Justice Mansfield used to sit in the House of Lords. He was born in Scone Castle in the year 1705, and died in 1793, in his eighty-ninth year.

————

The family of the Earl of Mansfield, who holds the hereditary feofeeship of the Palace of Scone, derives from Sir William Murray, of Tullibardine, who died in 1511.

29 0067

WHITLEY COURT,

NEAR DROITWICH, WORCESTERSHIRE.—EARL OF DUDLEY AND WARD.

WHITLEY or Witley Court, for the word is spelled both ways, was also in more ancient times written Whitlege, Whittleg, and Veceloge. At one time it belonged to the Cookseys, an old family of the county of Worcester, and was carried from them, through an heiress of the estate, into that of the Russells of Strensham.

From them it was purchased by Thomas Foley, Esq., of whom Nash, the historian of Worcestershire, observes, "This family is a striking instance what great riches may be acquired in a trading county by integrity, industry, frugality, and an extensive trade, and this within four generations. Bishop Fleetwood says, the law hath laid the foundation of two-thirds of all the honours and great estates in England: more than this proportion may be reckoned in Worcestershire. In all England there is no noble family, and very few opulent ones, that sprang from the church, except Lord Sandys. All our late war, glorious and successful as it was, hath not yet ennobled one soldier, (February, 1776.) Physick hardly ever raised its professors above knighthood or baronetage. Our county, besides a Foley, can shew a Knight, a Taylor, and others who have gained a more than ministerial fortune by the iron-trade, and attention to their own domestic affairs; while on the other hand, a Wild, a Tracey, a Lane, and many others, have spent large estates in elections and hunting for court favours."

From the family of Lord Foley the place passed by sale to Lord Ward.

The parish church adjoins the house; and Sulivan, author of the "Tour through England," writes thus of it in the second volume of that work. "The church, which is annexed to the house, is really an elegant building; the whole of it is beautified at a great expense; the sides white and gold, the ceiling divided into handsome compartments, with good Scripture pieces, and the glass windows exquisitely painted by an artist of the name of Price, who executed them in the year 1719. Uncommonly handsome as this edifice is, it still carries a disadvantage which those who are not uncommonly orthodox would dislike. It, unfortunately, is the parish church, so that the graves and tombstones are absolutely in the area of the house. This I mentioned to the old lady who conducted us through the apartments; but she, shaking her head, and staring at me with surprise, very calmly replied, that, if people are shocked at the sight of mortality, it is very easy for them to shut the windows."

The old lady was right. If there are "sermons in stones," as it has been well said that there are, even in those that we walk upon in every road, surely most of all in those which, whether speaking in the "storied urn and animated bust," or in those more plain and homely ones which chronicle in every "Country Churchyard" where underneath the green turf the "rude forefathers of the hamlet sleep," give one and the same lesson to all who survive but for a time, till their own turns shall come.

The family of Lord Dudley is derived from William Ward, a wealthy goldsmith of London, Jeweller to Henrietta, Queen of Charles I.

WHITLEY COURT.

GLASLOUGH PARK.

GLANUSK PARK,

NEAR CRICKHOWELL, BRECKNOCKSHIRE.—BAILEY, BARONET.

GLANUSK PARK, in South Wales, was at one time the property of Lord Orford, and was afterwards owned by Mr. John Keppel, from whom it passed in the present century into the hands of Joseph Bailey, Esq., M.P. for the city of Worcester.

The present imposing mansion was built by Mr. Bailey, on the existing site, the previous house being thought to be too close to the so-called Glanusk Water, in consequence of which it was taken down.

The park, which is well stocked with deer, comprises between seven and eight hundred acres of ground, exceedingly beautiful from its undulations, and is surrounded by mountains.

The River Usk, whereof Glanusk forms a part, runs for several miles through the estate, affording abundance of salmon and trout to the fisherman, as well as adding not a little to the beauty of a landscape which, from the mixture of wood, dale, rock, and meadow, presents a most romantic picture.

Within the park are some ancient Druidical remains, which have, as may be supposed, given ground for a variety of speculations to the learned in antiquities, but these would be unsuited to the pages of a work like the present.

The family of Bailey derives from John Bailey, Esq., of a family long resident in Yorkshire. His son,

SIR JOSEPH BAILEY, was created a Baronet in June, 1852. He married first, October 10th., 1810, Maria, daughter of Joseph Latham, Esq., by whom he had, with other issue,

JOSEPH BAILEY, Esq., M.P. for the County of Hereford, who married, June 22nd., 1839, Elizabeth Mary, only child of William Congreve Russell, Esq. He died August 31st., 1850, and left, with other children,

SIR JOSEPH BAILEY, who succeeded as second Baronet on the death of his grandfather, November 20th., 1858, and married Mary Ann, eldest surviving daughter of Henry Lucas, Esq., M.D., of Glan-yr-afon.

Sir Joseph Bailey, the first Baronet, was left a large fortune by his uncle, Richard Crawshay, Esq., of Cyfartha Ironworks, Glamorganshire, who died in 1810, which has been increased by his extensive ironworks at Nant-y-Glo. He was also possessed of considerable landed property in the counties of Brecon, Radnor, Glamorgan, Monmouth, Hereford, and Bucks., in several of which are handsome seats of his. He represented the city of Worcester in three Parliaments, and sat latterly for Breconshire. He was High Sheriff of Monmouthshire in 1823, and was a Deputy Lieutenant for that county and Breconshire, and was in the Commission of the Peace for the counties of Brecon, Glamorgan, Monmouth, and Hereford. He was patron of eight livings. He died November 20th., 1858, at Glanusk.

BURTON-AGNES HALL,

NEAR BURLINGTON, YORKSHIRE.—BOYNTON, BARONET.

THIS very fine and interesting specimen of an English gentleman's country-seat is situated in the East-Riding, on a gentle eminence at the edge of the Yorkshire Wolds, commanding an extensive view over Holderness and the level lands at the foot of the hills just mentioned. It has a south aspect, and is a good example of the style of architecture which was prevalent in the reigns of Queen Elizabeth and King James the First. It is said to have been built after a design by Inigo Jones. The house is of brick, with stone quoins.

There are some very fine rooms within, elegantly fitted up, and containing a good collection of family portraits and other paintings.

The entrance-hall is very large and lofty, and the chimneypiece is elaborately carved with figures of the wise and foolish virgins. There is a magnificent screen carried up to the top of the room, and richly ornamented with a mass of the most delicately-traced carving. It was brought here from Barmston, a neighbouring village and lordship belonging to the family.

A staircase of quaint design leads up to the "Long Gallery," which has a coved ceiling in imitation of a bower of trellis-work, intertwined with roses and creeping plants. There are some pictures on the panel-work said to be by Rubens.

In front of the house is a massive gateway, with four small octagonal towers.

In the space between it and the hall is a statue of a Gladiator.

The Parish Church is close to the mansion, and has several very elegant monuments of the families of Somerville and Griffith, one of them of alabaster, on which are the effigies of a knight and his lady, and above it a window of richly-decorated stained glass of recent manufacture.

The family of Boynton is stated to derive from

BARTHOLOMEW DE BOYNTON, (Boynton is an adjoining parish at the other side of the Wolds,) living in 1067, who was an ancestor of

MATTHEW BOYNTON, Esq., who married Anne, daughter of Sir John Bulmer, of Wilton, and was succeeded by his son,

SIR THOMAS BOYNTON, M.P. for Boroughbridge and High Sheriff of Yorkshire in the reign of Queen Elizabeth. He was succeeded by his son,

SIR FRANCIS BOYNTON, High Sheriff in 1596. This gentleman married Dorothy, daughter and co-heiress of Christopher Place, Esq., of Halnaby, and dying April 9th., 1617, was succeeded by his only surviving son,

SIR MATTHEW BOYNTON, Knight, of Barmston and Boynton, who was created a Baronet May 25th., 1618. Sir Matthew sat in Parliament in the reign of Charles I., and sided with the republicans during the civil wars. He married, first, Frances, daughter of Sir Henry Griffith, Knight, of Burton-Agnes, in Yorkshire, sole heiress of her brother, Sir Henry Griffith, Baronet, (a family now long extinct in the male line,) and thus brought Burton-Agnes into the Boynton family.

BALMORAL CASTLE,*

NEAR BALLATER, ABERDEENSHIRE.—THE ROYAL PRIVATE RESIDENCE.

THE assertion may safely be hazarded, that until Balmoral became the property of the Queen, or rather, in the first instance, of the Prince Consort, His Royal Highness Prince Albert, not one person in every hundred thousand in this country, or perhaps a smaller proportion, had ever even heard the name of the place. Now it is one of the "household words" which has become "familiar in our ears."

The property long belonged to the family of

FARQUHARSON of Invercy, in whose possession it had long been. It was let on lease in the year 1836 by the then proprietor, to Sir Robert Gordon, brother of the Earl of Aberdeen, for a period of thirty-eight years, and a shooting lodge was built by him on the estate. In the year 1848 Prince Albert bought of him the remainder of the lease, and in the year 1852 purchased the property from the trustees of the Earl of Fife. The new castle was then erected as a residence in the north for the royal family, who have since made it their favourite resort.

It is situated on the bank of the river Dee, and looks on one side up the valley to the west, and on another southwards to the foot of Craig-an-Gowan, and in the distance to the deer forest of Ballochbowie.

Windsor Castle commenced this volume, and being in one sense the property of the nation, and its associations of world-wide interest, I gave a full account of its varied features and historical contents. But Balmoral being altogether the Queen's own private property, it would perhaps be more proper to leave Her Majesty in the undisturbed enjoyment of that retirement which she so greatly loves, and which the author of the present work feels, with her, is the greatest earthly blessing that can be enjoyed, and especially as to be had in the northern parts of our island, the blessing of peace and quiet in the country.

* See View on the Title.

THE

County Seats

OF THE

Noblemen and Gentlemen

OF

GREAT BRITAIN AND IRELAND.

EDITED BY

THE REV. F. O. MORRIS, B.A.,

Rector of Nunburnholme, Yorkshire.

AUTHOR OF A "HISTORY OF BRITISH BIRDS," DEDICATED BY PERMISSION TO HER MAJESTY THE QUEEN.

"It is a reverend thing to see an ancient castle or building not in decay, or to see a fair timber tree sound and perfect; how much more to behold an ancient family which hath stood against the waves and weathers of time."—*Bacon*.

LONDON:
LONGMANS, GREEN, AND CO., PATERNOSTER ROW.

NOTICE.

A SERIES OF

PICTURESQUE VIEWS OF

OF

Noblemen and Gentlemen

OF

GREAT BRITAIN

VOL. II.

LEEDS
D. BANKS, QUEEN STREET

COUNTY SEATS

OF THE

NOBLEMEN AND GENTLEMEN

OF

GREAT BRITAIN AND IRELAND.

EDITED BY

THE REV. F. O. MORRIS, B.A.,

AUTHOR OF A "HISTORY OF BRITISH BIRDS," DEDICATED BY PERMISSION TO HER MAJESTY THE QUEEN.

VOL. II.

LONDON:
LONGMANS, GREEN, AND CO., PATERNOSTER ROW.

CONTENTS.

THE COUNTY SEATS.

ALNWICK CASTLE,

ALNWICK, NORTHUMBERLAND.—DUKE OF NORTHUMBERLAND.

HERE was, as is supposed, a Roman fortress, for, writes Grose, "when a part of the castle keep was taken down, under the present walls were discovered the foundations of other buildings, which lay in a different direction from the present, and some of the stones appeared to have Roman mouldings. The fretwork round the arch leading to the inner court is evidently of Saxon architecture, and yet this was probably not the ancient entrance, for, under the Flag Tower, before that part was taken down and rebuilt, was the appearance of a gateway that had been walled up, directly fronting the present outward gateway into the town."

Later on it belonged to

WILLIAM TYSON, a Saxon baron slain at the battle of Hastings, whereupon his daughter and her lands were both bestowed by William the Conqueror upon

IVO DE VESCY, one of his companions in arms. The last of his race,

WILLIAM DE VESCY, left it by will to

ANTHONY BEC, Bishop of Durham, in trust for his son, then a minor, but after seven years, namely, in the year 1310, the bishop sold it to

HENRY, LORD PERCY, predecessor of the present family.

This grand baronial castle was besieged in 1093 by Malcolm the Third, King of Scotland, but he being unexpectedly attacked by Robert de Moubray, a potent Norman baron, his army was totally defeated, Canmore himself being killed in the battle. In memorial of this event a cross was erected on the spot where he fell, which, after having fallen into decay, was restored in the year 1774 by the then Duchess of Northumberland, Her Grace being herself descended from Malcolm, through his daughter Maude, Queen of Henry the First of England.

II.

In 1174 it was again laid siege to by William the Third of Scotland, who was taken prisoner; which is also commemorated by a monument.

In the lapse of ages afterwards the wear and tear of time worked their natural ravages on this ancient pile, which had stood so long the "battle and the breeze," when, on the death of

JOCELINE PERCY, eleventh EARL OF NORTHUMBERLAND, his heiress,

LADY ELIZABETH PERCY, became in her own right Baroness Percy, and, by her second (or third?) marriage, to Charles Seymour, Duke of Somerset, had an only surviving child and heiress,

LADY ELIZABETH SEYMOUR, who wedded, in 1740,

SIR HUGH SMITHSON, BART., ancestor of the Dukes of Northumberland.

———

The family of Smithson is stated to derive from John Smithson, living in 1446; that of Percy descended from William de Percy, one of the Norman companions of the Conqueror in 1066.

BEAUDESERT,

NEAR LONGDON, STAFFORDSHIRE.—MARQUIS OF ANGLESEY.

BEAUDESERT in former times belonged to the Bishops of Lichfield, but was granted by King Edward the Sixth to Sir William Paget, Knight, ancestor, in the female line, of the present family. Quaint old Fuller gives the following account of him:— "William Paget, Knight, was born in the city (London,) of honest parents, who gave him pious and learned education, whereby he was enabled to work out his own advancement. Privy Counsellor to four successive princes, which, though of different persuasions, agreed all in this—to make much of an able and trusty Minister of State. 1. King Henry VIII. made him his secretary, and employed him ambassador to Charles the Emperor and Francis King of France. 2. King Edward VI. made him chancellor of the duchy, comptroller of his household, and created him Baron of Beaudesert. 3. Queen Mary made him keeper of her Privy Seal. 4. Queen Elizabeth dispensed with his attendance at court in favour of his great age, and highly respected him. Indeed, Duke Dudley in the days of King Edward ignominiously took from him the garter of the order, quarelling that by his extraction he was not qualified for the same. But if all be true which is reported of this Duke's parentage, he of all men was most unfit to be active in such an employment. But no wonder if his pride snatched a garter from a subject, when ambition endeavoured to deprive two princes of a crown. This was restored unto him by Queen Mary, and that with ceremony and all solemn accents of honour, as to a person 'who by his prudence had merited much of the nation.' He died very old Anno 1569; and his corps (as I remember) are buried in Lichfield, and not in the vault under the church of Drayton, in Middlesex, where the rest of the family, I cannot say *lye* (as whose coffins are erected) but are very compleatly reposed in a peculiar posture which I meet not with elsewhere."

The mansion is finely placed on the side of an eminence, well sheltered by rising grounds, and environed by woods and timber.

It is of brick and stone, with two projecting wings.

It was erected in the reign of Queen Elizabeth, but has since then had many alterations and additions.

Within the house is a noble gallery ninety-seven feet in length, by seventeen in width.

The dining-room is large, with a vaulted ceiling, and otherwise richly ornamented.

The drawing-room is fifty-two feet long, by twenty-seven wide.

The library contains a valuable collection of books, and some manuscripts, and among the latter a curious Register of Burton Abbey.

The park abounds with deer, and the walks and pleasure-grounds on all sides of the house are considered to fully justify the title of Beaudesert.

Dr. Plot, the historian of Staffordshire, gives an account of some repeating echoes which are to be heard here, and says, "they are as good, or perhaps better than any in Oxfordshire; there being one at Beaudesert, in a little park about the middle of the path that leads from the *pale* to the *house*, that from a treble object answers distinctly three times."

On the top of the hill behind the house there are traces of a large encampment, called Castle Hill. "It is elevated so high above all the country near, that it commands the horizon almost all round, whence, it is said, may be seen the nine several counties of Stafford, Derby, Leicester, Warwick, Worcester, Salop, Chester, Montgomery, and Kent." This last-named, however, I conceive there must be some mistake about.

Cannock Chase, or Cannock Forest, is on the border of the estate, and here is found the cannel coal of which Dr. Plot writes:—"The cannel coale is the hardest, and of so close a texture that it will take a passable polish, as may be seen in the choir of the Cathedral Church of Lichfield, which in great part is paved lozeng, black and white (as other churches with marble) with cannel coale for the black, and alabaster for the white, both plentifully found in this country; which, when kept clean, so well represent black and white marble, that to an incurious heedless eye they seem to be the same. It turns like ivory into many pretty knacks, such as ink-boxes, candlesticks, etc. They cut it also into salts, standishes, and carve coats of armes in it; witness that of the Right Hon. William Lord Paget in the gallery of his stately seat at Beaudesert. This coal is dug in the park adjoining, also belonging to his lordship, about twenty, thirty, or sometimes forty fathoms deep, lyeing between other beds of a softer kind, and is the best in Staffordshire, or anywhere else that we know of, except that in Lancashire, which (they say) has no grain, and therefore no cleaving, as this will doe, upon which account esteemed somewhat better for making such utensils as were mentioned above; and yet this at Beaudesert will work so very well that the King's Majestie's head is said to have been cut in it by a carver at Lichfield, resembling him well." The name of cannel coal is considered to be equivalent to candle coal, from the light flame which it emits; but I cannot help thinking that it comes of the same origin as the word Cannock, the place where it is found, unless indeed on the other hand, being of very ancient extraction, it may have given the name to the locality, abbreviated from candle-coke into can-coke, and so Cannock.

———

The family of Paget, which descended from William Paget, one of the Sergeants at Mace of the City of London, but is now extinct in the male line, is derived paternally from the Right Reverend Lewis Bayley, Bishop of Bangor, tutor to King Charles the First, and Chaplain to his brother Henry Prince of Wales, son of King James the First.

BELVOIR CASTLE,

NEAR GRANTHAM, LEICESTERSHIRE.—DUKE OF RUTLAND.

ROBERT DE TODENI, Standard-bearer to the Conqueror, was the original grantee of Belvoir, and erected a Norman fortress on the site of the present castle. His successors assumed the name of

ALBINI, and from them the place passed by descent to the family of

LORD ROS, of Hamlake, whose eventual heiress,

ELEANOR DE ROS, conveyed it by marriage to

SIR ROBERT MANNERS, M.P., ancestor of the Earls and Dukes of Rutland and of Lord de Ros.

I cannot do better than transcribe the following account of the princely mansion of Belvoir:—

"It would be long to tell the various mutations that Belvoir Castle underwent before the erection of the present stately edifice. In the feudal times, in the Wars of the Roses, and in the troubled times of Charles I., it was frequently garrisoned; its commanding military position naturally rendering it a station of great importance. At the commencement of the present century, successive attempts at modernizing had nearly reduced the style and character of the castle to that of an ordinary hall. When the present noble Duke came to his majority one of his first objects was the rebuilding the castle of his ancestors, or rather, restoring it to its appropriate character. At an outlay of £200,000 this great work had nearly been completed in 1816, when, on the 26th. of October in that year, a fire broke out, which reduced the magnificent structure to a blackened ruin. Portions, however, of the castle escaped the devouring element, as the south-west and the south-east fronts, and the beautiful chapel. At the time of this conflagration the castle contained collections of works of art and *vertù* that could scarcely be surpassed by any private mansion in Europe. Many valuable pictures by the old masters were consumed, and much of the costly furniture destroyed.

To this brief sketch of the castle it is right to add some description of its accessories. At a short distance are the faint traces of the ruins of the Benedictine Priory of Belvoir, founded *temp.* Gi. Conquestoris. Below the castle rock begin romantic walks, leading through groves and thickets to the delightful pleasure-grounds. These grounds, with all their appropriate adjuncts of statue, grotto, fountain, and bower, may be said to have been the creation of the late Duchess, to whose fine and exquisite taste they appear to be consecrated. A pillar, standing on her favourite spot, bears a touching poetic tribute to her loveliness and worth. A gentle ascent from this charming *pleasaunce* leads to the family mausoleum, in which her earthly remains repose.

Mention ought to be made of the imposing effect which the castle has when viewed from any portion of the adjoining domain. In this it greatly surpasses Windsor. The rich masses of wood that flank it, its more numerous towers, and its more commanding site, combine indeed to give it a proud pre-eminence over all other English castles.

. Belvoir Castle forms the subject of a remarkable Pindaric ode of great length, first printed in 1690, and reprinted in Nichols' 'Leicestershire.' It also forms the theme of a Latin poem of great merit, entitled 'Arx Belvoirina,' in a collection of the poems of Louth school by the Rev. Andrew Burnaby. The poet Crabbe, who held the neighbouring living of Muston, has also celebrated the castle and its inmates in his nervous strains."

———

The family of the Duke of Rutland derives from Sir Robert de Manners, Knight, ancestor of Sir Robert de Manners, Knight, living in the reign of Edward the Second.

HATFIELD HOUSE,

HATFIELD, HERTFORDSHIRE.—MARQUIS OF SALISBURY.

———

In consequence of Hatfield having been from time to time intimately connected with the lives of those who have occupied the most distinguished positions in the annals of our country, it has become of unusual interest. I cannot, however, do more than briefly allude to some of its more prominent historical associations.

Hatfield is a place of great antiquity, at one time forming part of the revenue of the Saxon kings. It remained in their possession until the time of

EDGAR, by whom it was bestowed upon the monks of Ely. They held the estate till the year 1109, when Henry the First converted the monastery of Ely into a bishopric. Hatfield then became the residence of the prelates of that see, and was hence distinguished by the title of Bishop's Hatfield.

During the reign of Henry the Seventh the house was rebuilt by Morton, Bishop of Ely, but shortly afterwards was exchanged by Bishop Godrick with Henry the Eighth.

It continued the property of the crown till the fourth year of James the First, when it was exchanged for the palace of Theobalds with

SIR ROBERT CECIL, whose successors have continued to hold it up to the present time.

EDWARD VI. made Hatfield his residence during his father's reign, and from it he was conducted to the throne.

ELIZABETH also kept her state here for the last few months of Edward's reign, and again under the guardianship of Sir Thomas Pope, during the four years preceding her accession to the throne, and at the death of her sister she was proclaimed queen before the gates of Hatfield.

Elizabeth's court here appears to have been attended with magnificent displays, one of which is thus described by a contemporary writer:—"In Shrovetide 1556 Sir Thomas Pope made the Ladie Elizabeth all at his own costes a great and rich maskinge in the great halle at Hatfelde: when the pageants were marvelously furnished. There were there twelve minstrels antickly disguised; with forty-six or more gentlemen and ladies, many of them knights or nobles and ladies of honour, aparelled in crimsin satten embrothered uppon with wrethes of golde, and garnished with bordures of hanging perle. And the devise of a castell of clothe of gold, sett with pomegranates about the battlements, with shields of knights hanging therefrom, and six knights in rich harneis turneyed. At night, the cuppboard in the halle was of twelve stages, mainlie furnished with garnish of gold and silver vessels and a banket of seventie dishes, and after a voidde of spices and suttleties with thirty spyse plates, all at the chardgis of Sir Thomas Pope; at the next day the play of 'Holophornes;' but the Queen Mary percase misliked these folleries, as by her letters to Sir Thomas Pope hit did appear, and so their disguisinge was ceased."

The house as it now stands, or nearly so, was built by Sir Robert Cecil in the year 1611; he did not, however, long survive the completion of this work, for he died the next year, worn out with business and anxiety.

The following account of the mansion is given by Clutterbuck in his "History and Antiquities of the County of Hertford:"—"This house, which is a fine specimen of the domestic architecture of the period in which it was erected, is situated in a park of considerable extent, watered by the River Lea, and sheltered on the north by stately avenues of elms and oaks of venerable growth. The building is constructed of brick and stone, in the shape of an oblong, surmounted by a lofty clock, with wings projecting from the south front, flanked at their corners with square towers. Along the whole length of the front runs a Doric collonade supporting a gallery, divided into two equal parts by a frontispiece of three stories, in the Doric, Ionic, and Corinthian orders. In the third story of this frontispiece is a stone shield, on which are sculptured the arms of Cecil, Earl of Salisbury, with their quarterings, encircled by a garter, and supported by two lions, underneath which is the family motto, 'Sero sed Serio,' and above, in the open balustrade which runs along the top of the front, under the crest and coronet, is the date 1611.

The interior of the mansion is laid out in a style of magnificence corresponding with its exterior. On the right of the principal entrance there is a spacious and lofty hall, furnished on its eastern side with a minstrels' gallery, enriched with carved pilasters and pannels, and set with figures of beasts and grotesque ornaments characteristic of the fashion of the times in which it was erected."

Hatfield House continues to sustain its reputation for being honoured with the presence of royalty, inasmuch as Queen Victoria was a visitor here in 1846, and in the present year, 1867, the Queen of Holland became the guest of the Marquis of Salisbury.

———

The family of Cecil derives from Richard Cyssel, an officer in attendance at the court of Henry the Eighth.

HAMPTON COURT,

THE descent of this ancient place is as follows:—

The first structure was erected in the reign of Henry the Fourth, (by whom the first stone is recorded to have been laid,) by

SIR ROWLAND LENTHALL, Master of the Wardrobe to His Majesty, and who married Margaret, daughter and co-heiress of Richard Fitz-Alan, K.G., Earl of Arundel, Warren, and Surrey, and the house is said to have been furnished with spoils from the field of Agincourt. Upon his death the estate devolved on females, his cousins, and after being sold to

LORD BURFORD, (CORNEWALL,) it afterwards became, by purchase, the property of

SIR HUMPHREY CONINGSBY, Knight, one of the Justices of the Court of King's Bench in the reign of Henry the Eighth. He left by his wife Cicely, daughter and co-heiress of John Salwey, Esq., of Stanford, in Worcestershire, a son and heir,

HUMPHREY CONINGSBY, ESQ., who had issue by his wife Anne, daughter of Sir Thomas Inglefield, Knight, one of the Judges of the Court of Common Pleas, two sons and three daughters, of whom the surviving son and heir,

SIR THOMAS CONINGSBY, was knighted by Queen Elizabeth in 1591. He died May 30th., 1625, having married Philippa, daughter of Sir William Fitzwilliam, of Milton, in Northamptonshire, Lord Deputy of Ireland, and had ten children, of whom the youngest son,

FITZWILLIAM CONINGSBY, became next of Hampton Court, and was Sheriff of the County in 1627. He married Cicely, daughter of Henry Nevile, seventh Lord Abergavenny, and by her was father of

HUMPHREY CONINGSBY, who married Lettice, eldest daughter of Arthur Loftus, Esq., of Rathfarnham, in Ireland, and had an only son,

THOMAS CONINGSBY, ESQ., who was an active participator in the revolution which brought in William the Third, and at the Battle of the Boyne was so close to the king that he staunched a wound on his shoulder grazed by a bullet. The handkerchief he used is still preserved with great care in the library. In consideration of his eminent services His Majesty constituted him and Henry, Lord Sydney, Lords Justices of Ireland, and in the year 1693 created him

LORD CONINGSBY of Clanbrassil, in the county of Armagh, and he was sworn a Member of the Privy Council in England. On the accession of George the First he was raised to the Peerage of England as a Baron of Great Britain, by the title of

II.   C

Lord Coningsby of Coningsby, Lincolnshire, June 8th., 1716, with limitation to his daughter Margaret, a singular limitation, as he had a son by a former wife. He was also appointed Lord Lieutenant of Herefordshire. He married first Barbara, daughter of Ferdinando Gorges, of Eye, in the same county, by whom he had

THOMAS CONINGSBY, ESQ., who, by his wife, daughter of John Carr, Esq., of the county of Northumberland, was father of

RICHARD CONINGSBY, second Lord Coningsby of Clanbrassil, who dying without male issue on the 18th. December, 1729, the title became extinct. He had by his second wife, Frances, daughter of Richard Jones, Earl of Ranelagh, a son,

RICHARD CONINGSBY, who died young, and two daughters,

> LADY MARGARET CONINGSBY,
>
> LADY FRANCES CONINGSBY.

Of whom the elder was created in 1716

VISCOUNTESS CONINGSBY of Hampton Court, and succeeding her father in 1729, became

COUNTESS OF CONINGSBY, and married, in 1730, Sir Michael Newton, K.B., son of Sir John Newton, Baronet, of Barrs Court, in Gloucestershire, but died in 1761 without issue. The younger daughter,

LADY FRANCES CONINGSBY, married Sir Charles Hanbury Williams, K.B., son of John Hanbury, Esq., of Pontypool, by whom she left two daughters, co-heiresses,

> FRANCES,
>
> CHARLOTTE.

The younger,

CHARLOTTE HANBURY WILLIAMS, married William Anne Holles Capel, Earl of Essex, who inherited the estate from his grandmother, and sold it in the year 1817 to

RICHARD ARKWRIGHT, ESQ.

The present magnificent seat, built near the site of one of the most celebrated old mansions in the kingdom, stands in an extensive park and grounds adorned with stately timber, and with beautiful views in every direction, the two rivers, Lugg and Arrow, meandering through the estate, till they meet together near the house.

The principal front, (on the east side of which is the chapel,) of most imposing appearance, is towards the north. In the centre is a massive square tower. Over the entrance is a panel, sculptured with the arms and supporters of the Coningsbys, which are also painted on some old glass, with the dates 1613 and 1614.

Within the house in many of the apartments are a number of fine paintings, and also much of the ancient furniture still preserved.

————

The family of Arkwright derives from Richard Arkwright, born at Preston, in Lancashire, in 1732, the celebrated inventor of improvements in the machinery used in the cotton manufacture, for which he received the deserved honour of knighthood as Sir Richard Arkwright.

MULGRAVE CASTLE,

————

THE situation of Mulgrave Castle is extremely fine, commanding a magnificent view of the German Ocean, on which one looks through precipitous banks in the grounds, as if on a picture set in a frame.

In the times of old it was a fortress of a Saxon Duke, by name

WADA, whom tradition has handed down as a giant.

In subsequent Norman times the castle and barony were granted to

NIGEL FOSSARD, from whose family it was next conveyed by the marriage of the heiress with

SIR ROBERT DE TURNHAM, in the reign of Richard the Lion-hearted. He dying without a male heir, his daughter,

ISABELLA DE TURNHAM, having become, by the death of her father, a ward of the crown, was given in marriage by King John to

PETER DE MALO LACU, otherwise called Peter de Mauley, a native of Poictou, and esquire to the king, who had engaged him to assassinate Prince Arthur, to clear the way for his own accession to the throne.

To this Peter, succeeded, according to Camden, seven others of the same Christian name in succession, until the reign of Henry the Fifth, when the estates were conveyed by an heiress into the family of

BIGOD, and next, by another, into that of

RADCLIFFE.

Subsequently, namely, about the year 1625, the property went into the hands of

EDMUND, LORD SHEFFIELD OF BUTTERWICK, Lord President of the North, who, in the reign of Elizabeth, had greatly distinguished himself by many gallant actions, and more particularly in assisting towards the defeat of the Spanish Armada. He was created by King Charles

EARL OF MULGRAVE, but the family became extinct in 1735. The title was, however, again revived in the person of

CONSTANTINE PHIPPS, whose grandmother on the mother's side, Catherine, Dowager Countess of Anglesey, had re-married, secondly, John Sheffield, Duke of Buckingham, and by his bequest had succeeded to the Mulgrave and other estates. The son of the above,

CONSTANTINE JOHN PHIPPS, the second Lord, distinguished himself as an arctic voyager, by reaching to a far higher latitude than any of his predecessors.

Jet is found in the neighbouring cliffs between Mulgrave and Whitby, of which Solinus quaintly says, "In Britain there is great store of gagates, or jet, a very fine stone. If you ask the colour, it is black and shining; if the quality, it is exceeding light; if the nature, it burns in water, and is quenched with oil; if the virtue, it has an attractive power when heated with rubbing."

The family of Lord Normanby derives from Sir William Phipps, who received the honour of knighthood from King James the Second. He was a distinguished mathematician, and the inventor of the diving bell, by means of which he was successful in recovering an immense treasure from the wreck of a Spanish galleon. He was afterwards appointed Governor of Massachusetts.

WOBURN ABBEY,

NEAR WOBURN, BEDFORDSHIRE.—DUKE OF BEDFORD.

———

HERE was in early times a monastery of the Cistercian order, founded in the year 1146 by

HUGH DE BOLEDAC, a powerful baron, incited to the work, it is recorded, by the Abbot of Fountain's Abbey, Yorkshire.

These abbey lands were given by King Edward the Sixth, after the dissolution of the monasteries, to

JOHN, LORD RUSSELL, soon afterwards created Earl of Bedford, in whose family they have remained ever since.

The building, as may be supposed, has been variously altered from time to time. The present mansion was built by the fourth duke.

The principal front is of the Ionic order of Grecian architecture, and was the work of the fifth duke.

The Venetian Drawing-room has a fine series of twenty-four views of Venice, by Canaletti, from which it derives its name.

In the hall is a mosaic pavement removed from Rome.

There is a sculpture gallery one hundred and thirty-eight feet long by twenty-four feet wide, with a flat dome over its centre supported by eight marble columns, containing a fine collection of antique marbles, among which is the famous Lante Vase of Parian marble, six feet three inches wide, and six feet high, inclusive of the pediment on which it stands, with two magnificent handles, and beautifully sculptured. It was found in the ruins of Hadrian's villa at Tivoli, of which no doubt it formed a conspicuous ornament. Also a fine cast of the Apollo Belvidere, a statue of Psyche, by Westmacott, and sculptures of Bacchus, a bust of Fox, etc., etc.

The state bedchamber is most magnificently furnished.

The picture-gallery has a number of fine portraits of the Russell family, and among the best are those of William Earl of Bedford, the Countess of Somerset, and Lady Catharine Brooke.

Woburn Abbey was visited by Queen Elizabeth in the year 1572, and by King Charles the First in 1645.

Within the last few years upwards of three hundred model cottages have been built on the estate, for the tenantry, by the Duke of Bedford.

The park is extensive and well timbered, and is surrounded by a wall eight feet high.

———

The family of Russell is of French origin, deriving originally, as is stated, from the Du Rozells of Normandy, and in later times from John Russell, Constable of Corfe Castle in 1221.

RABY CASTLE,

NEAR STAINDROP, DURHAM.—DUKE OF CLEVELAND.

THIS splendid edifice has in part continued from Anglo-Saxon times, but it was principally erected in the year 1379, by

JOHN DE NEVILLE, with whose potent descendants it continued, until, in an unfortunate moment,

CHARLES NEVILLE, sixth and last Earl of Westmoreland, (of that family,) engaged in a conspiracy against Queen Elizabeth. It failed altogether, her good fortune standing her in good stead, as it did on so many other occasions, and he escaped only with his life, and fled to the Netherlands, where he died an exile in the year 1584. His immense estates were declared forfeited, and in the reign of James the First the castle and demesne of Raby were purchased by

SIR HENRY VANE, Knight, whose grandson,

SIR CHRISTOPHER VANE, was created Baron Barnard, of Barnard Castle, in the county of Durham. His descendant,

HENRY, LORD BARNARD, was raised to the higher title of Viscount Barnard and Earl of Darlington, by King George the Third, April 3rd., 1754; and again his grandson,

WILLIAM HENRY, the third Lord, was elevated in the year 1833 to the Dukedom of Cleveland.

The park and pleasure grounds of this splendid place are such as might be expected, woods, hills, and valleys giving an endless succession of beautiful views.

The Castle itself stands on about two acres of ground, and at irregular distances are two towers, respectively designated the Clifford Tower and the Bulwer Tower.

The hall is of noble proportions, and the roof is arched, and supported on six columns, which diverge and spread over the ceiling.

Above the hall is a large and grand room, ninety feet in length by thirty-four wide, in which the baronial feasts were used formerly to be held, and where no fewer than seven hundred knights who held of the Nevilles are recorded to have been entertained on one occasion.

Leland considered Raby as the "largest castle of logginges in all the north country."

The late Countess of Darlington made a curious collection of objects of natural history in a museum at Raby Castle; a happy taste, suitable to a period of peace and tranquillity; how great an advance on the troublous times of the Nevilles.

12 VIII 68

The family of the Duke of Cleveland is stated to be derived from a Welsh ancestor, Howell ap Vane, who lived long before the Conquest, and more immediately from Sir Henry Vane, knighted for his valiant deeds at the battle of Poictiers, 19th. September, 1356.

HARLAXTON MANOR,

NEAR GRANTHAM, LINCOLNSHIRE.—GREGORY.

HARLAXTON was once upon a time a hunting seat of John of Gaunt, "time-honoured Lancaster," and as it is not far from Melton Mowbray, the head quarters of the chase, the coincidence is remarkable enough, though it is scarcely to be supposed that the pursuit has been kept up continually in the district ever since.

The old Manor House was taken down not many years ago, and the present splendid mansion erected in its stead.

There was a bequest left to the parish by Cadwallader Gwynne, Esq., the interest of which is paid yearly to the poor.

The late American ambassador to England, Mr. Everett, wrote of his own country, "We have everything great in America. We have great rivers, great mountains, great forests, and great lakes; but we have no olden buildings, no castles or houses of an ancient aristocracy, and no monasteries. To see these we must visit the land of our fathers." "There is something," says Sir Bernard Burke, "equally just and beautiful in this affectionate tribute to the old country, and the more so kind and ennobling a feeling spreads amongst the Americans, the better it will be for themselves. Abstractedly there is no great value in uninhabitable ruins, and no doubt a mere utilitarian would look upon the finest Gothic cathedral as a mere stone receptacle for bones and dust, which would be more profitably employed in manuring our fields; but somehow there is a feeling, in all save the obtusest of us, that will be heard in spite of utilitarianism, and we shall invariably find that whatever tends to connect us in idea with the past or future, tends also—and in a greater degree than anything else save revealed religion—to make us conscious that we belong not wholly to the earth or to the present, but are portions of immortality. He who narrows his thoughts and wishes to the time being, may certainly reap some practical advantage from this limited application of his faculties, but it will be at the expense of higher and better feelings."

"An interest of a very peculiar kind attaches to the castles, mansions, and baronial halls of England, of which every class, in its own degree and after its own fashion, is alike sensible. With the uneducated, as a mass, this generally appears linked with the supernatural, or with deeds of violence and bloodshed; the man of imagination has the same feeling, but under a higher and more fanciful aspect. 'To distract the mind,' says Dr. Johnson, 'from all local emotion, would be impossible if it were endeavoured, and would be foolish if it were possible. Whatever withdraws us from the power of our senses; whatever makes the past, the distant, or the future predominant over the present, advances us in the dignity of thinking beings. Far from me and my friends be such frigid philosophy as may conduct us, indifferent and unmoved, over any ground which has been dignified by wisdom, bravery, or virtue. That man is little to be envied whose patriotism would not gain force upon the plain of Marathon, or whose piety would not grow warmer among the ruins of Iona.' "

"To the modern mansions belong attractions of an equal amount, but of a different nature. The most republican disposition has a natural, and, we may therefore infer, a praiseworthy curiosity to become acquainted with the site of great actions, and the habits of illustrious characters. This kind of interest cannot fail to hang around most of our country halls and mansions. Those who possess them are men placed in a position commanding either a general or a local reputation; not infrequently combining both. It is wonderful to see what a strong hold these seats of the great and wealthy have upon the minds and affections of all who dwell in the same county. No doubt those in humble situations do not always view with complacency the better fortunes of others; but with this for the most part mingles a vague feeling that the honour of their country is involved in the great men and noble seats that adorn it, and that that honour is in some manner their own. To all this must be added the beauty of the landscapes in which our halls and mansions are placed, a beauty of a kind that may be considered peculiar to England, where nature has been cultivated, not superseded, while in other countries the scenery is altogether wild or altogether artificial. Those who are insensible to such considerations may perhaps find their imaginations more pleasantly stirred by the pictures, busts, relics, and curiosities that almost ever abound in the seats of our territorial proprietors."

The family of Gregory derives from

JOHN LONGDEN, ESQ., whose son,

JOHN LONGDEN, ESQ., was father of

JOHN LONGDEN, ESQ., who took the name of SHERWIN in 1818, and again in 1860 the additional one of

GREGORY, on succeeding to the Harlaxton estate at the death of George Gregory, Esq.

ARDTULLY,

NEAR KENMARE, KERRY.—ORPEN, (KNIGHT.)

———

THOUGH scarce a vestige of the castle, on the site of which the present residence at Ardtully has been built, now remains, the ancient title might still continue to attach to it, as in the similar case of Castle Howard, already mentioned in the present work, where the name alone remains as a record of the past, without a single trace of the original building, and the same in several other like instances, but the present member of the family, into whose possession it has come, has discontinued it on raising the new edifice.

There are, however, as presently stated, a few mouldering relics of the former towers of Ardtully still in being, which may serve to summon up before the mind's eye the wild times so long passed away, when it stood firm as a fastness among the mountains; and again those long intervening years, when, before the utter ruin that followed, the words of the poet might still have been applicable to them:—

> "The roofless cot, decayed and rent,
> Will scarce delay the passer-by;
> The tower by war or tempest bent,
> While yet may frown the battlement,
> Demands and daunts the stranger's eye:
> Each ivied arch and pillar lone
> Pleads haughtily for glories gone."

Ardtully, the country seat of Sir Richard John Theodore Orpen, is beautifully situated at the confluence of the rivers Roughty and Obeg, in the valley of Glenarough, about five miles east of the town of Kenmare, in the county of Kerry. It is built on the site of an ancient castle, belonging to the family of Mc Finnin Mc Cartie, who forfeited in the rebellion of 1641. He would appear from his name and character to have been the prototype of the modern Fenians, so that one might have supposed that they are nothing new after all, and that thus history repeats itself: it is, however, stated that the word means "the Son of Florence," but I fancy I have somewhere seen the other derivation, and can only say to my readers, "utrum horum mavis accipe." There had been previously, on the same spot, an abbey called "Monaster ni Oriel," of which mention is made in "Archdall's Monasticon." It has been suggested that the abbey may have been founded by some monks from Oriel in

Ulster, the people of which were, as mentioned in the "Annals of Innisfallen," called in Irish *Oirgialla Olltach*. Ardtully is called Ardentully in "Pacata Hibernia."

The waters of the rivers Roughty and Obeg being there contracted between rocks on either side, the flood rises to a great height; from whence, it is said, is derived the name Ardtully, in Irish *Ardtuilè*, that is "High flood." The monastery has entirely disappeared, but some carved stones of the castle remain. It seems to have been a place of considerable strength.

The Orpen family settled in Kerry in the time of the second Charles, having lost their property in England in consequence of their adherence to that monarch's father, King Charles the First.

The Orpens claim descent, through Sir John Orpen, from Monsieur Erpen de Seulli or Saulier, who came to England with the Conqueror. They also claim to be of the same family as that of Sir Thomas Erpingham, of Erpingham, or Orpingham, in the county of Norfolk, the hero of Agincourt. The family subsequently resided at a place called the "White House," about a mile from the town of Kenmare, built in a strong position on the river of that name. This house, now in ruins, is celebrated for the siege, which Mr. Richard Orpen of that day and the Protestants of his neighbourhood, sustained against the troops of James the Second, as mentioned in the last volume of Lord Macaulay's "History of England."

A branch of the above-named Orpen family settled at Ardtully about one hundred and fifty years since, from whose descendants it passed into the hands of

Sir Richard John Theodore Orpen, who built the house represented by the plate, on the site of the old mansion where previously had stood Ardtully Castle.

The family of Orpen is connected with that of the editor of the present work, by the marriage of his father, the late Rear Admiral Henry Gage Morris, R.N., of York, and afterwards of Beverley, with Miss Rebecca Newenham Millerd Orpen, daughter of the Rev. Francis Orpen, B.A., vicar of Kilgarvan and rector of Dungourney, in the county of Cork.

ELVASTON CASTLE,

NEAR DERBY, DERBYSHIRE.—EARL OF HARRINGTON.

THOUGH there does not appear to have ever been a castle on the site of the residence at present under our notice, nor any feature of the building that can lay claim to such a title, yet it has been well observed that as in England every man's house is said to be his castle, so that world-wide saying gave an undoubted right to the Earl of Harrington, who built this so-called castle, to give it that designation if it pleased him to do so.

The estate of Elvaston is situated about five miles from the town of Derby.

It was first settled by Sir John Stanhope, father of the Earl of Chesterfield, on the eldest son of his second marriage.

In the year 1643 the old hall was held by his widow, when Sir John Gell, the Parliamentarian, with his forces besieged and plundered it. He further proceeded to the church and destroyed a tomb, on the effigy of which Lady Stanhope had expended £600., and then wantonly rooted up her ladyship's flower-garden. Strange to say, his next step was to marry the lady herself, for the express purpose, as is stated, of "destroying the glory of her husband and his house." Probably no more effectual mode of doing so could have been resorted to than a union with one who presented so great a contrast to the gallant and loyal spirit of her departed husband.

In the year 1817 important alterations were made in the castle. The Gothic hall that forms the entrance was begun, and it is furnished with a series of valuable specimens of ancient armour.

There are several very fine apartments, among which may be mentioned a dining-room, drawing-room, and library. Gilding has been extensively brought into requisition, even the statuary being ornamented with it.

"With the exception of the wondrous gardens at Alton Towers, those at Elvaston stand unrivalled. The Allanton process of transplanting full-grown trees has been very successfully practised, under the direction of Mr. Barrow, the head gardener. Every beautiful tree for miles round has been brought to Elvaston, with as much ease as Birnam Wood came to Dunsinane, and the result is such an *arboretum* as no other nobleman's seat can shew. Gilded statuary, interspersed among these, has the rich effect which green and gold always produce. Water, too, has been made by machinery a great auxiliary to the beauty of the scene. Beautiful, however, as Elvaston gardens confessedly are, they were, during the late Earl's time, entirely shut up from the public. Even his lordship's own tenantry could not gain admittance.

The present more liberal-minded Earl has shewn a better feeling, and so great has been the desire of the public to avail themselves of the new privilege, that it was suggested that some security against the great influx of people was absolutely necessary. Special days have therefore been fixed upon, and a small sum charged for admittance, which is generously devoted to the county charities. The sums realized have been considerable; and it is not unusual on these public days to see several thousands enjoying the beauties of this enchanting scene. The river Derwent bounds the domain on the north. The adjoining church, covered with ivy, and containing several fine monuments, is well worth a visit. A few years ago it was hung with those rustic funeral garlands of which Derbyshire has retained the last trace."

The family of Lord Harrington derives from Sir Richard Stanhope, living in the reign of Henry the Third.

MILTON ABBEY,

NEAR BLANDFORD, DORSETSHIRE.—HAMBRO, (BARON.)

"Non cuivis adire" so sweet a spot as that in which Milton Abbey is situated, standing as it does in a sequestered valley, or rather where three valleys meet, on a gracefully undulated lawn, surrounded by hills on every side, themselves adorned with woods to their top.

Milton, or Middleton, of which the former name is a contraction, lies in the very centre of the county of Dorset; the middle town of the shire.

According to the Domesday Book the manor of Middleton belonged, at the time of the Conquest, to an abbey thus designated, which had been founded by the Saxon King Athelstane.

The Conqueror seized all church lands held in frank almoigne, and then granted them by knights' service in chief, so as thus to insure the submission and fealty of his vassals.

In the reign of Henry the Eighth, when the monasteries were dissolved, Milton Abbas, as the demesne was then called, in common with many other abbey lands in the county, as for instance Cerne Abbas—a contraction, I should suppose, of the word Abbacy—was granted to

JOHN TREGONWELL, Esq., in consideration of the sum of £1,000, and the relinquishment of a pension of £40 a year, to be held in chief by knight's service, as the tenth part of a knight's fee. To him succeeded his son

— TREGONWELL, who compounded for his estate by a fine of £3,735, deserting the Parliament, and residing in the king's quarters.

The last of the family,

JOHN TREGONWELL, Esq., left a daughter, an heiress,

MARY TREGONWELL, who married first

FRANCIS LUTTRELL, Esq., and secondly, after his decease,

SIR JACOB BANCKS, a native of Sweden, who dying in 1724 left it to his son,

JACOB BANCKS, Esq., at whose death, in 1737, without a will, the possession of the property was contested by several parties, the principal of whom was Mr. Tregonwell, who claimed as heir to Mr. Bancks on his mother's side, and Mr. Strachan, who claimed in like manner on the father's side. The affair was ultimately compromised, and the estate remained in the possession of

— STRACHAN, Esq., who sold it in the year 1752 to

JOSEPH DAMER, Esq., created Baron Milton and Earl of Dorchester in the year

1792.   He had been successively Member of Parliament in 1741 for Weymouth and Melcombe Regis; in 1747 for Bramber; in 1754 for Dorchester.   He was afterwards made a Privy Councillor, and was raised by King George the Third to the Peerage of England, by the style and title of Baron Milton, of Milton Abbey, in the county of Dorset.   He built the present mansion about the year 1771, and laid out the grounds with great taste.   The park wall extends five miles in length, and the drives through the plantations extend more than ten miles.   His descendant,

LORD PORTARLINGTON, again alienated the property by sale to

BARON HAMBRO, a Danish nobleman.

The Abbot's Hall is the only part of the old monastery that remains, and is in its original state, being fifty-three feet six inches long, and twenty-six feet six inches wide.   The roof is of Irish oak, finely wrought; a stone pilaster supports it, and bears the date of 1498, the time no doubt of its erection.   On a bordering of stone work that runs across the wall are the arms of several ancient families on stone shields. At the lower end of the hall is a carved wooden screen, and near the upper end an oriel nineteen feet four inches long, and fourteen feet eight inches broad.

The drawing-room contains some fine paintings.

––––––

The family of Baron Hambro is, as above stated, of Danish origin.

13 MA68

TRINITY MONASTERY.

COBHAM HALL,

————

COBHAM, a very pleasant spot in Kent, gave its name to the head of a family which possessed it in the reign of King John, namely,

HENRY DE COBHAM, to whom it was assigned by William Quatre-Mere, a Norman soldier, in the first year of the above-named monarch's reign.

His line ended in the person of

JOHN, third LORD COBHAM, a gallant warrior in the reign of King Edward the First, who also earned more peaceful distinction by founding Cobham College. He died in 1467. His daughter,

JOAN COBHAM, married Sir John de la Pole, and their daughter,

JOAN COBHAM, endowed with the great inheritance of her grandfather, was married no less than five times, namely, in succession to

SIR ROBERT HERMANDALE,

SIR REGINALD BRAYBROOKE,

SIR NICHOLAS HAWBECK,

SIR JOHN OLDCASTLE,

SIR JOHN HARPENDEN.

By the four first she had children, all of whom however died young, excepting only the youngest (by Sir Reginald Braybrooke,) namely,

JOAN BRAYBROOKE, who became the heiress, and married

SIR THOMAS BROOKE, of Brooke, in the county of Somerset, a knight of good landed estate. Of their fourteen children, ten sons and four daughters, the eldest son

JOHN (BROOKE) LORD COBHAM, a distinguished soldier under Edward the Fourth, was great grandfather of

WILLIAM (BROOKE) LORD COBHAM, K.G., Warden of the Cinque Ports, Ambassador to the Low Countries, Lord Chamberlain, and Governor of Dover Castle, who entertained Queen Elizabeth in one of her well-known "progresses" through Kent. He died in 1596, having left money for the building and endowment of a new College on the site of the one founded by his ancestor in the year 1362. His eldest son

HENRY (BROOKE) LORD COBHAM, succeeded his father as Lord Warden of the Cinque Ports, but having joined with his brother George Brooke in the alleged treason of Sir Walter Raleigh, was condemned with the former to death. His brother, however, alone was executed, he having escaped by an ignominious confession, which, though it saved his own inglorious life, was the ruin of Raleigh. The only excuse that can be

II.   E made for him is that he was a person of weak and almost imbecile mind—a mere tool in the hands of more wily conspirators. Upon his attainder, his possessions were granted to the crown by Act of Parliament, and James the First gave the estate of Cobham Hall, to

LUDOVICK STUART, DUKE OF LENNOX, who, though he was thrice married, left no children, and was succeeded by his brother,

ESME STUART, LORD AUBIGNY, who had married Catherine, daughter and heiress of Gervas, Lord Clifton, and died within a year after succeeding to the estate, leaving a son,

JAMES, DUKE OF LENNOX AND RICHMOND, K.G., who died in France when only ten years old, when his titles and estates devolved on his cousin-german,

CHARLES STUART, EARL OF LICHFIELD, K.G., Ambassador to the Court of Denmark, who died there in 1672. His sister and heiress was

LADY KATHERINE STUART, who afterwards became Baroness Clifton, in right of her grandfather. She was married twice, first to Lord Henry O'Brien, of the princely House of Thomond, and secondly to Sir Joseph Williamson, one of the principal Secretaries of State. The latter purchased the Manor of Cobham of the Duke of Lennox and Richmond. He died in 1701, and left two thirds of his estates to his widow, which at her death, the November following, devolved on her grandson,

EDWARD LORD CORNBURY, only son of Edward Hyde, Earl of Clarendon, by the daughter of Lord Henry O'Brien, named above, and at his demise in 1703, passed to his sister,

LADY THEODOSIA HYDE, who in the following year wedded

JOHN BLIGH, ESQ., M.P., afterwards created Earl of Darnley. The remaining third of the estate after prolonged lawsuits, which in the end were compromised, became vested in the Bligh family.

The park and grounds of Cobham are extensive and well wooded, and several huge and ancient oaks and chesnuts are conspicuous for their size and girth, one of the latter especially, known by the name of the "four sisters" measures more than thirty feet in circumference, and has been described and figured in Mr. Strutt's work. One avenue leading from the village consists of a double row of lofty lime trees, and is a fine example of the old-fashioned plan.

The mansion itself is described as a splendid specimen of the Tudor style of architecture. The last Duke of Richmond and Lennox added a centre to the ancient building; the two wings on either side of it having been erected by the then Lord Cobham, in 1582.

The late Lord Darnley also spared neither expense nor time in restoring the character of the whole place.

———

The family of Lord Darnley descends from William Bligh, of Plymouth, living about the year 1600.

ALLERTON PARK,

NEAR KNARESBOROUGH, YORKSHIRE.—LORD STOURTON.

ALLERTON PARK is situated in the parish of Allerton Mauleverer, between four and five miles to the east of Knaresborough, in the West Riding of the county of York.

Together with the hamlets of Clareton and Hopperton, the parish consists of about two thousand three hundred acres of land, mostly the property of Lord Stourton, the Lord of the Manor.

The park itself consists of about four hundred acres. It is described by Bigland, in his "Beauties of England and Wales," as "charmingly picturesque, presenting a great variety of hills, dales, and groves, delightfully interspersed, and a beautiful lake contributes to ornament the scenery. On a lofty eminence, finely shaded with trees, is an octagonal tower, consisting of two rooms, the first thirty-six feet by twenty, the second twenty feet by fifteen. The entrance is by a double flight of steps, both of which, as well as the terrace round the building, are secured by iron palisades. From this commanding situation are seen to the greatest advantage the variegated landscapes of the park, together with extensive views of the surrounding country."

The house is a handsome cemented building, in the Grecian style of architecture.

In ancient times the estate belonged to the family of

MAULEVERER. It next came into that of

LORD GALWAY, by whom it was sold to

HIS ROYAL HIGHNESS THE DUKE OF YORK, who again sold it in the year 1789 to

COLONEL THORNTON, who gave the house the name of Thornville Royal. It was finally sold in the year 1805, namely, the mansion, park, and estate, for the sum of £163,800, to

LORD STOURTON.

Here was formerly a Benedictine Priory, founded by one Richard Mauleverer in the reign of Henry the Second. It was bestowed at the dissolution of the monasteries on King's College, Cambridge.

The family of Lord Stourton arose from the town of Stourton, in Wiltshire, and flourished in that county before the Conquest, for it appears that one of those who most resolutely opposed the French invaders was

BOTOLPH STOURTON, who broke down the sea-wall of the Severn, and disputed every inch of ground, compelling the Duke to grant him his own terms, having entered Glastonbury when William made his appearance in the west.

From this gallant Briton descended

Sir Ralph de Stourton, father of

William de Stourton, whose son,

John de Stourton, was succeeded by his son,

William de Stourton, whose son,

Sir John Stourton, was a distinguished soldier and statesman in the reign of King Henry the Sixth, by whom he was raised to the peerage, May 26th., 1455, as

Baron Stourton, of Stourton, in the county of Wilts., ancestor of the family before us.

MELBURY HOUSE,

———

THIS ancient seat was originally the possession of the family of
SAMPFORD, who were Lords of the Manor. It afterwards belonged to the house of
MALTRAVERS, then to that of
STAFFORD, and next to the family of
STRANGWAYS, from whom it passed by marriage to that of
FOX (now FOX-STRANGWAYS.)

Here was in the olden time an ancient pile, and it is recorded by Leland that
Sir Giles Strangways "avaunced the inner part of the house with a lofty and fresche
tower." For this work he is stated to have brought three thousand loads of stone
from the Hampden quarry, nine miles distant.

The present house, which is one hundred feet square, stands upon a gentle
eminence, and occupies three sides of a quadrangle, respectively fronting east, north,
and south. Of these, that which fronts the east is the principal, and each is adorned
with pilasters of the Corinthian order. The path leading to the entrance is conducted
over a stone bridge of ten arches, that spans a fine sheet of water on the north
side of the mansion.

. There are many valuable portraits at Melbury, and also various ancient relics,
among them being a letter written by Oliver Cromwell, which runs as follows:—

> "For ye h^{ble} Coll.
> Edmund Whalley
> at his quarters
> haste these.

> "Sir,

> I desire you to be with all my troopes, and Collonel Hines his
troopes alsoe at Wilton at a Rendevous by break of day tomorrow morning, for we
heare the enemy has a designe upon our quarters tomorrow morning.

> "Sr. I am
> Yr Cozen and Servant
> OLIVER CROMWELL.

> "Sarum, Wednesday
> night at 12 o'clock."

The scenery around is thus described by Hutchins:—"The ground," he says, "around the mansion is diversified by nature in beautiful irregularity of hill and dale, of verdant pastures and venerable woods. Various trees, of great size and beauty, present themselves in every point of view. The oak and the elm distinguish themselves above the rest; of the former there is one whose circumference exceeds thirty-two feet. At a pleasing distance from the south front the canal extends itself into the shape and size of a majestic river, whose opposite bank is clothed with a numerous assemblage of lofty forest trees. These cover the base of a hill, whose summit rises over their tops, and extends in a delightful terrace to the east and west. Hence the eye traverses an immeasurable tract of country. On the east the bold prominence of Bub Down presents the first object, and at the distance of almost thirty miles in the same line, the entrenchments of Humbledon Hill and the town of Shaftesbury are distinctly seen. Proceeding northwards, Bradley Knoll, Alfred's Tower, Wells Cathedral, the Mendip range of hills, the wonderful chasm at Cheddar Cliffs, and other remarkable objects rise to view. On the north-west are the Quantock Hills; and to the west the eye catches the appearance of a forest, stretching to an immeasurable distance, whose utmost boundaries reach the clouds."

––––––––––

The family of Lord Ilchester descends from Sir Stephen Fox, a gallant and loyal cavalier living in the reign of King Charles the Second.

TAYMOUTH CASTLE,

NEAR ABERFELDY, PERTHSHIRE.—MARQUIS OF BREADALBANE.

———

THIS magnificent seat may well carry us back in thought to the feudal times, and even in them it would have been conspicuous for size, grandeur, and beauty.

The estate is no less than about a hundred miles long, and the castle is situated moreover in one of the most delightful valleys for which the Highlands of Scotland are so deservedly famous.

So regal a residence deserves a royal description, and the following lines by Queen Victoria are from Her Majesty's "Leaves from the Journal of Our Life in the Highlands:"—

"The drive was quite beautiful all the way to Taymouth. The two highest hills of the range on each side are (to the right, as you go on after leaving Dunkeld) Craig-y-Barns and (to the left, immediately above Dunkeld) Craigoinean. The Tay winds along beautifully, and the hills are richly wooded.

"Taymouth lies in a valley surrounded by very high, wooded hills; it is most beautiful. The house is a kind of castle, built of granite. The *coup d' œil* was indescribable. There were a number of Lord Breadalbane's Highlanders, all in the Campbell tartan, drawn up in front of the house, with Lord Breadalbane himself in a Highland dress at their head, a few of Sir Neil Menzies' men (in the Menzies red and white tartan,) a number of pipers playing, and a company of the 92nd. Highlanders, also in kilts. The firing of the guns, the cheering of the great crowd, the picturesqueness of the dresses, the beauty of the surrounding country, with its rich back-ground of wooded hills, altogether formed one of the finest scenes imaginable. It seemed as if a great chieftain in olden feudal times was receiving his sovereign. It was princely and romantic. Lord and Lady Breadalbane took us up stairs, the hall and stairs being lined with Highlanders.

"The Gothic staircase is of stone and very fine; the whole of the house is newly and exquisitely furnished. The drawing-room, especially, is splendid. Thence you go into a passage and a library, which adjoins our private apartments.

"The dining-room is a fine room in Gothic style, and has never been dined in till this day. Our apartments also are inhabited for the first time."

The deer park is very extensive, and is adorned with abundance of stately timber: there is an avenue of lime trees nearly a mile long.

Here was formerly an ancient castle, called Ballock, but only some remains of it are now extant. It was erected by Colin, sixth Laird of Glenurchy, who died there in the month of April, 1583.

The modern mansion was begun about the beginning of the present century. It stands upon the southern bank of the Tay, in a semicircular lawn about a mile below the termination of the lake, embosomed by woods that well-nigh seem interminable. It consists of a large quadrangle, with a circular tower at each corner, a lofty lantern tower in the centre, and an eastern wing one hundred and eight feet long, in which are comprised the offices. An arched cloister goes round the exterior on three sides, the tracery of which is exceedingly light and beautiful.

The principal rooms are the baron's hall, containing a large collection of books, the dining-room, the drawing-room, and the Chinese room. The grand staircase, in the florid Gothic style of architecture, rises to the full height of the central tower, being lighted above by long pointed windows, while galleries open below to the apartments in the higher storeys.

There are in the castle many valuable pictures by some of the great masters,— Titian, Annibale Carraci, Tintoretto, Castiglione, Teniers, Vandyke, Rembrandt, Leonardo da Vinci, Salvator Rosa, etc.

It has been well written, by one who viewed this splendid place under the right aspect, "Nothing can exceed the beauty and grandeur of the scenery of this princely domain. Wood and water, mountain, meadow, objects animate and inanimate, in endless variety, are here so blended, and on such a scale, that when viewed from certain positions, and in certain states of the atmosphere, they give you an impression as if you had been transported to a region of enchantment. But to speak becomingly, there is here the workmanship of far more than enchanter's ken, or enchanter's might:—

"Surrounded by His power we stand;
On every side we feel His hand.
Oh! skill for human reach too high,—
Too dazzling bright for mortal eye!"

The family of the Marquis of Breadalbane derives from Gillespick Campbell, living in the tenth century.

8 JU68

CHOLMONDELEY CASTLE,

NEAR MALPAS, CHESHIRE.—MARQUIS OF CHOLMONDELEY.

CHOLMONDELEY CASTLE is situated about four miles from Malpas, and about eight from Nantwich, in the county of Chester.

Here was an ancient hall, which in its turn was succeeded by another then modern one, built in the reign of Queen Elizabeth. Upon a carved beam were engraved the initials of Sir Hugh Cholmondeley, Knight, and Mary his wife.— S. H. C. M. C.

During the civil wars Cholmondeley House was used as a garrison, first by the Cavaliers, and then by the Roundheads. In the first instance the Parliamentarians attacked it, killed fifty of the Royalists, and carried off six hundred horses. On the 24th. of the same month the cavalry poured out of Cholmondeley and plundered Nantwich without mercy. In November the tide of war again turned, and the Cromwellians came into possession, but only to be summarily ejected by the king's troops, who, however, were again dislodged by the others, June 30th., 1644.

The facts are thus related by Burghall in his diary:—

"Sunday. They marched towards Cholmondeley House with three or four pieces of ordnance, and four cases of drakes, when two Nantwich companies, volunteers, guarding the great piece of ordnance, met them; and before break of day they planted all their great pieces within pistol-shot of the house, and about three or four in the morning, after they had summoned them, they played upon it, and shot through it many times; and they in the house shot lustily at them with their muskets. The besiegers, playing still on them with their ordnance and small shot, beat them at last out of the house into their works, where they continued their valour to the utmost, themselves being few, killing four or five more of them, and Major Pinkney, a brave commander; but being too weak to hold out any longer, about one in the afternoon they called for quarter, which was allowed; and Mr. R. Horton, captain of the horse, let down the drawbridge,"—it was moated round— "and opened the gates, when the Earl of Denbigh, Colonel Booth, and the rest entered, and took the captain and all the rest prisoners—about thirty-six—with their arms and provisions."

II.   F

A domestic chapel in Cholmondeley Castle has stood for more than five hundred and fifty years, the date of its erection being attested by the original grant.

———

The family of Lord Cholmondeley derives from
HUGH, BARON OF MALPAS, in Cheshire, whose son,
ROBERT, left a daughter and heiress,
LETTICE, who married Richard le Belward, and their son (or grandson) was
WILLIAM LE BELWARD, whose second son,
ROBERT LE BELWARD, having had the lordship of Cholmondeley bestowed on him by his father, fixed his residence there, and assumed his surname therefrom.

WORSLEY HALL,

NEAR MANCHESTER, LANCASHIRE.—EARL OF ELLESMERE.

———

ONE of the Crusaders, one of the earliest of them, by name ELIAS, or ELISEUS, the founder of the family of Worsley, is recorded to have held the manor of Workeslegh, or Workedlegh, so early as the time of the Conquest.

In Hopkinson's "Pedigrees of Yorkshire" we read of him, that "This Elias was seized of the manor of Workesley, now Worsley, about the Norman Conquest, A.D. 1066. He was of such strength and valour that he was reputed a giant, and in old scripts is often called Elias Gigas. He fought many duells, combats, etc. for the love of our Saviour Jesus Christ, and obtained many victories." He is stated to have met his death at Rhodes.

Worsley Hall, the present house, is a stately mansion built of brick, and stands on high ground which not only overlooks the extensive park attached to it, but commands a view of no fewer than seven counties.

It was built by Francis, Duke of Bridgewater, about the middle of the last century.

The old hall, with its pointed gables, seated on the site of the gardens belonging to the modern house, is described as "remarkable as the depository of a series of spirited grotesque and allegorical heads, with an intermixture of ornamented devices engraved in oaken panels, and brought within the present century from one of the state rooms of Hulme Hall, Manchester, one of the manorial mansions of the family of Prestwich. Many of the sculptured heads represent the domestic buffoons of the sixteenth century; others are suggested by religious mysteries. The costumes appear mostly of the fashion of the reigns of Henry the Seventh and Henry the Eighth."

Sir Walter Scott expressed the highest admiration in inspecting drawings of these heads by Captain Jones.

The Roman antiquities discovered in recent times at Castlefield are preserved at Worsley Hall.

———

The family of the Earl of Ellesmere deduces its descent, in the male line, through the family of the Duke of Sutherland, from

SIR ALLAN GOWER, Lord of Stittenham, in Yorkshire, High Sheriff of the County at the time of the Conquest, (or, by others, from William Fitz Guyer, of Stittenham, living in 1167.)

In the female line it derives from

ALEXANDER, eleventh Earl of Sutherland, whose descendant,

WILLIAM, seventeenth earl, had an only daughter,

ELIZABETH, married to George Granville, Marquis of Stafford, and their son was

GEORGE GRANVILLE, second Duke of Sutherland.

SWITHLAND HALL,

NEAR MOUNTSORRELL, LEICESTERSHIRE.—EARL OF LANESBOROUGH.

———

SWITHLAND HALL is situated in a lordship of that name, containing about one thousand and eighty acres of land.

It is situate two miles from Mountsorrell, five from Loughborough, and seven from Leicester, south of Woodhouse.

In the time of King Henry the Third this manor was the inheritance of

SIR WILLIAM DE WALLIES, with whose posterity it continued until the reign of Richard the Second, when it passed by marriage to

SIR JOHN DE WALCOTE, Knight. It subsequently became the property of

SIR JOHN DANVERS, whose daughter wedded the

HONOURABLE AUGUSTUS RICHARD BUTLER, second son of the Earl of Lanesborough, who thereupon, as below referred to, assumed the name of DANVERS.

———

The family of Lord Lanesborough derives from

JOHN BUTLER, of Waresley, in Huntingdonshire, whose descendant,

SIR STEPHEN BUTLER, settled in Ireland in the reign of King James the First. He died in 1639, and was succeeded by his eldest son,

JAMES BUTLER, ESQ., of Belturbet, whose brother,

STEPHEN BUTLER, ESQ., M.P. for Belturbet, married Anne, daughter of the first Lord Santry, and was followed by his eldest son,

FRANCIS BUTLER, ESQ., M.P. for Belturbet, whose eldest son,

THEOPHILUS BUTLER, ESQ., created Baron of Newtown-Butler, was succeeded by his brother,

BRINSLEY BUTLER, second baron, Gentleman-usher of the Black Rod, and Colonel of the Battle-axe Guard in Ireland, who represented the county of Cavan in Parliament, and was made Viscount Lanesborough on the 12th. of August, 1728. Ho had twenty-three children, five only of whom survived infancy, and his eldest son,

HUMPHREY BUTLER, second Viscount Lanesborough, was raised to the earldom in 1756, and his son,

BRINSLEY BUTLER, second Earl of Lanesborough, had with other issue,

AUGUSTUS RICHARD BUTLER, the second son, who married Elizabeth, daughter and heiress of Sir John Danvers, Bart., when he assumed the additional name and arms of Danvers, and his eldest son,

GEORGE JOHN DANVERS BUTLER-DANVERS, became of Swithland Hall.

CLIFTON HALL,

NEAR NOTTINGHAM.—CLIFTON, BARONET.

CLIFTON HALL stands on a rocky eminence by the side of the "Silver Trent," which gently meanders beneath, and the grounds are adorned with extensive plantations.

The road to the house from Nottingham is through an avenue of fine trees a mile in length.

Here, according to tradition, the "Clifton Beauty" was hurled down the precipice by her lover, into the river below; and such a legend has, as might readily be supposed, since made the spot attractive to those who have been disposed to go there on a similar errand; I do not mean for the tragical issue.

The present mansion was more than twelve years in re-building.

There is a charming terrace in the gardens, commanding some most delightful views of home scenery.

The cliff on which the house stands is of alabaster, curiously inlaid in many places with a beautiful spar, which glitters brightly in the sunshine, in contrast to the dark marl with which it is commingled.

The name of this ancient family is derived from Cliffe-ton, or Clifton, a small hamlet on a cliff or eminence about two miles from the town of Nottingham, which in the reign of Edward the First was the property of

JOHN DE SOLENI, and was purchased from him by

SIR GERVASE DE CLIFTON, Knight, Sheriff of Nottinghamshire and Derbyshire in 1279 and the six following years. In 1286 he was appointed High Sheriff of Yorkshire, which post he also filled for six years. His descendant was

SIR JOHN CLIFTON, M.P. for Nottingham in 1403, who married Catherine, daughter of Sir John de Cressy, of Hodsack, and sister and co-heiress of Sir Hugh de Cressy, and was slain at the battle of Shrewsbury, fighting for the king. His lineal successor,

ROBERT CLIFTON, a gentleman of martial character, who lived in no fewer than four reigns, those namely of Henry the Eighth, Edward the Sixth, Mary, and Elizabeth, was great-grandfather of

GERVASE CLIFTON, ESQ., created a Baronet May 22nd., 1611, ancestor, through

SIR GERVASE CLIFTON,

SIR WILLIAM CLIFTON,

SIR GERVASE CLIFTON,

SIR ROBERT CLIFTON,

SIR GERVASE CLIFTON,

SIR ROBERT CLIFTON,

SIR JUCKES GRANVILLE JUCKES-CLIFTON, of

SIR ROBERT JUCKES CLIFTON, who succeeded as ninth Baronet in 1852.

12 AU 68

STOWE PARK,

STOWE, in local language, means, it is said, an eminence or rising ground, and hence to this place its name.

The house, which was originally designed, it is stated, by Lord Camelford and Lord Cobham, is in the Grecian style of architecture, with a centre of four hundred and fifty-four feet, which, with the two wings, makes the whole front nine hundred and sixteen feet in length, including the chapel.

Within the mansion, the oval saloon is sixty feet long by forty-three wide and fifty-six high; the hall dining-room fifty feet by thirty-two feet; the gallery seventy feet by twenty-five; and the state bedchamber fifty feet by thirty-five.

A stately avenue of two miles long leads from the town of Buckingham, about two miles distant, to the park, at the entrance of which is a Corinthian arch sixty feet high.

Within the grounds the principal objects of note are, a cedar tree twenty-two feet in girth; a column erected in honour of Captain Grenville, who fell in a sea-fight against the French, under Lord Anson, in 1747; a monument to Captain Cook; the Temple of Ancient Virtue, containing many statues; the Queen's Temple, in honour of Queen Charlotte, 1789; the Palladian Bridge; the Temple of Friendship, erected by Lord Cobham to receive the busts of his political friends; the Gothic Temple; the Bourbon Tower, surrounded by trees planted by Louis the Eighteenth; a column, one hundred and fifteen feet high, surmounted by a statue of Lord Cobham; the Temple of Concord and Victory, built by Lord Cobham *in memoriam* of the Seven Years' War, and in front of it are some oak trees planted by Queen Victoria on occasion of her visit to Stowe in 1845, and two cedars by Prince Albert. "There is a charming flower-garden, thickly surrounded by high trees, firs, cedars, evergreens, and flowering shrubs."

Stowe was formerly an abbey, and on the dissolution of the monasteries was granted by King Henry the Eighth to

ROBERT KING, the first Bishop of Oxford, who had been Abbot of Osney, and to his successors in the see.

It was afterwards surrendered by the then Bishop to the crown, and was granted in the year 1500 to

THOMAS COMPTON and another, by whom it was immediately conveyed to

JOHN TEMPLE, ESQ., whose son,

II.

SIR THOMAS TEMPLE, was created a Baronet in 1612. His descendant,

SIR RICHARD TEMPLE, was highly distinguished in the wars under the Duke of Marlborough in the reign of William the Third, and, on the accession to the throne of King George the First, was made Baron Cobham, of Cobham, in the county of Kent, and further advanced in the year 1718 by the title of Viscount Cobham.

On his death the title of Baronet went to a younger branch of the family. His second sister, Mrs. Grenville, became Viscountess Cobham, and was soon afterwards made Countess Temple.

Her eldest son,

RICHARD, EARL TEMPLE, died without issue, and was succeeded by his nephew,

GEORGE GRENVILLE, who was created Marquis of Buckingham. In 1799 the then possessor of the title,

RICHARD GRENVILLE NUGENT CHANDOS TEMPLE, was made Earl Temple of Stowe, and in 1822 Duke of Buckingham and Chandos.

The ducal family of Buckingham, now represented by Richard Plantagenet Campbell Temple Nugent Brydges Chandos Grenville, the present Duke, derives from a family of the last-mentioned surname living at Wootton-under-Barnwood, in the county of Buckingham, in the reign of Henry the Fifth, and more immediately from Richard Grenville, Esq., who succeeded to the estates in 1618. He was followed in succession by

RICHARD GRENVILLE, ESQ.

RICHARD GRENVILLE, ESQ.

RICHARD GRENVILLE, first EARL TEMPLE, K.G., P.C., etc.

GEORGE GRENVILLE, second EARL TEMPLE, created in 1784 MARQUIS OF BUCKINGHAM.

RICHARD GRENVILLE, second MARQUIS OF BUCKINGHAM, further raised in the peerage as MARQUIS OF CHANDOS and DUKE OF BUCKINGHAM AND CHANDOS, father of the above-mentioned second Duke.

COMBERMERE ABBEY,

NEAR WHITCHURCH, SHROPSHIRE.—VISCOUNT COMBERMERE.

HERE was originally, as is conveyed by the name, an Abbey of Benedictine Monks, founded by one Hugh de Malbank in the year 1133.

When the dissolution of the monasteries took place, in the reign of King Henry the Eighth, that monarch bestowed the lands on George Cotton, who derived his family name from Cotton, or Coton, in the county of Salop, where they had been settled before the Norman Conquest, or from a village of that name in Cheshire. He was Esquire of the Body to His Majesty, Privy Councillor and Vice Chamberlain to Prince Edward. Thereupon the family quitted their residence in Shropshire for that which has since been their head-quarters in the county of Cheshire.

The mansion stands on the bank of a lake or mere, from which it derives its name, and occupies the site of the old monastery, of which some remains are still in existence.

The library has been adapted from the refectory, which in its original state was sixty feet long and twenty-eight feet high. The ancient oak roof is still preserved, and is richly ornamented with the carvings which were customary at that day. Upon the walls are the quarterings of the Cotton family from the time of King John, as also those of Salusbury, of Llewenny, now represented by Lord Combermere.

In the library there is a collection of valuable paintings, and many portraits of the Cottons.

The house is situated in the midst of a fine park. The Duke of Wellington planted in it the "Wellington Oak" when on a visit to his old companion in arms, Lord Combermere.

The family of Lord Combermere derives from Sir George Cotton, living in the reign of King Henry the Eighth, whose descendants were as follows:—

RICHARD COTTON, ESQ.

GEORGE COTTON, ESQ.

THOMAS COTTON, ESQ.

SIR ROBERT COTTON, BARONET.

SIR THOMAS COTTON, BARONET.

SIR ROBERT SALUSBURY COTTON, BARONET, M.P.

Sir Lynch Salusbury Cotton, Baronet.

Sir Robert Salusbury Cotton, Baronet, M.P.

Sir Stapleton Cotton, Baronet, G.C.B., G.C.H., G.T.S., K.S.F., K.S.I., who for his eminent military services in Spain and India was raised to the peerage as Baron, and afterwards Viscount Combermere.

Sir Wellington Henry Stapleton Cotton, second Lord Combermere.

———

Of this family was also that most truly excellent man, the Rev. Richard Lynch Cotton, D.D., successively Fellow, Tutor, and Provost of Worcester College, Oxford, within whose "classic shades" the writer of these pages received his university education.

LEEDS CASTLE,

NEAR MAIDSTONE, KENT.—WYKEHAM-MARTIN.

———

THIS remarkably fine seat is surrounded by a wide moat, containing nearly twelve acres of water, and the buildings themselves occupy about three acres more.

The original castle was built by

ROBERT DE CREVECŒUR, on whom it was bestowed by William Rufus. It was, however, ere long forfeited to the crown, and came into the possession of

WILLIAM DE LEYBORNE, by whom it was surrendered to the king, the donor making, as it should seem, a merit of necessity. It was next granted by the then king to

LORD BADLESMERE, who ungratefully joined the Earl of Lancaster in his attempt to put down the royal favourite, Piers Gaveston. As if this was not enough cause of offence, his wife, Lady Badlesmere, refused the demand of Queen Isabella for hospitality at the castle for one night, and some of the royal servants were killed in endeavouring to force an entrance. Edward in consequence besieged the castle, took it after a severe encounter, hanged the castellan, and committed Lady Badlesmere and her family to the Tower. The next year Lord Badlesmere himself shared the fate of his subordinate, and was hanged at Blean, near Canterbury, his head being then struck off, and fixed upon Bargate in that city.

The damage which the castle had sustained during the siege was repaired by Walter de Wykeham.

In the reign of Henry the Fifth, the monarch imprisoned here his mother-in-law, Joan of Navarre, for her traitorous attempt against his life.

Here, too, the Duchess of Gloucester was tried for witchcraft and sorcery.

At a later period the manor was granted by King Edward the Sixth to

SIR ANTHONY ST. LEGER, K.G., Lord Deputy of Ireland, and his son,

SIR WARHAM ST. LEGER, sold it to

SIR RICHARD SMYTH, who died there in the year 1628, and his daughters and coheiresses alienated the castle to

SIR THOMAS COLEPEPER, of Hollingbourne, whose descendant,

THE HONOURABLE CATHERINE COLEPEPER, married

THOMAS, fifth LORD FAIRFAX, of Cameron, whose successor,

ROBERT, seventh LORD FAIRFAX, had the honour of entertaining George the Third at Leeds Castle, and on his death in 1793, the property devolved, in default of direct heirs, on his lordship's nephew,

THE REV. DENNY MARTIN, whose successor,

GENERAL PHILIP MARTIN, was followed in the possession of the estate by his kinsman,

FIENNES WYKEHAM, ESQ., who assumed the additional surname of his predecessor, and was father of the next owner,

CHARLES WYKEHAM-MARTIN, ESQ.

The oldest part of the castle, as it appears at present, is the cellars, erected probably in the time of Henry the Third. At one period there was a Norman entrance to them, formed by a plain semicircular work of Caen stone, but which was covered up in 1822, when the southernmost of the two great divisions of the castle was pulled down and rebuilt. A drawbridge originally supplied the means of communication between the old castle and this part of the building; but it was long ago replaced by timbers fixed and floored, which, at the time of the alteration just mentioned, were in their turn taken away, and a stone bridge of two arches substituted in their place. Some parts of the building date unquestionably from the reign of Edward the First, others from that of Edward the Third, and a very great portion was built by Sir H. Guldeford in the reign of Henry the Eighth.

––––––––

The family of Wykeham-Martin deduces from Richard Wykeham, Esq., of Swalcliffe, living in the early part of the eighteenth century, (representative of the ancient house of which was Sir Ralph Wykeham, in the time of King John, and William of Wykeham, the founder of Winchester College and New College, Oxford,) father of

THE REV. ROBERT WYKEHAM, whose son,

FIENNES WYKEHAM, ESQ., assumed the additional surname of Martin in 1821.

GOPSAL HALL,

NEAR TWYCROSS, LEICESTERSHIRE.—LORD HOWE.

THIS well-known and magnificent seat is acknowledged to be one of the chief ornaments of the county of Leicester, in which it is situated.

It is about three miles north-west of Market Bosworth, and stands in a park of nearly six hundred acres. It was originally built by Charles Jennens, Esq., in the year 1758, at a cost of £100,000 when completed.

"The south front has an extremely imposing aspect. Corinthian pillars support a frieze and balusters of very graceful design, while a receding pediment bears in relief a sculpture of a ship in a storm, with a haven in the foreground, and the appropriate inscription, *Fortiter occupa portum.* This beautiful addition to the architectural features of Gopsal was introduced to commemorate the naval victories of Lord Howe. The wings of this front form, respectively, the chapel and library.

The principal entrance is on the north.

The whole of the interior is a combination of elegance and comfort too seldom found in the mansions of the nobility.

The library contains a very fine collection of rare works. A fine stained glass window, the painting of which was executed by the late Baroness Howe, is a much admired ornament of this splendid room.

The chapel may vie with any private chapel in England, either in chasteness of design or appropriateness of fitting. Every portion of the woodwork is of cedar of Lebanon, save the carved legs of the Communion Table, which are formed of the Boscobel oak. Vandyke's painting of the Crucifixion adorns the chapel, and the hall abounds in choice works of the old masters."

It was here that Handel composed his "Messiah," and it is stated to have been very much owing to the then proprietor of Gopsal that that noble composition was given to the world.

An intelligent tourist, T. R. Potter, Esq., gives the following account of this place:—"Every step you take at Gopsal shows that the arts have been not only fostered but cultivated here. Every walk in the neighbouring parishes, portions of this splendid domain, shows some church, bede-house, or school, erected and supported by the munificence of the Curzons, while the numerous tenantry and peasantry on the estates show, both by their appearance and their conduct, how much their welfare is the object of their landlord's solicitude."

Mr. Jennens died in the year 1773, and devised the estate to the Honourable Penn Assheton Curzon, his grandnephew, who wedded Lady Sophia Charlotte Howe, who became at the decease of her father, Baroness Howe, and so brought that title into the family of Curzon.

The family of Lord Howe derives in the male line from

GIRALINIE DE CURZON, living about the time of the Conquest, who held the manor of Locking, in Berkshire, and that of Fishead, in the county of Oxford.

DUNROBIN CASTLE,

———

The following is the account of this castle of the "far north," given by Sir Bernard Burke, in his "Visitation of Seats:"—

"Dunrobin Castle was first built by Robert, Earl of Sutherland, in the year 1275. It stands nearly in the middle of the parish of Golspie, upon the edge of a bank that rises considerably above the level of the sea. The building is of that old-fashioned style of Scotch architecture which defies classification, but which at the same time has a picturesque interest that does not always belong to more legitimate edifices. Narrow towers, tapering off like spires, and much lower than the building itself, flank either end, while the numerous windows look out quaintly from the dark and irregular mass.

The adjacent landscape is varied and hilly, with no want of timber; and the garden, which spreads itself out at the foot of the eminence on which the castle stands, harmonizes well with the character of the castle and its grounds, which have been vastly improved by the present noble proprietor."

The tower or castle of Dunrobin, even still existing, was reputed to be the oldest manse in Scotland.

The present mansion was designed and commenced in the year 1845. The style is, in the main, that of the old English baronial castle.

The successive Earls of Sutherland have added to their possessions generation after generation, and they now comprise the whole of what is called the Red Country, and also the estate and parish of Assynt, which was forfeited to the crown by the attainder of the Earl of Seaforth, and was sold to William, eighteenth Earl of Sutherland. It is a wild district of mountain and moor. The whole consists of eight or nine hundred thousand acres, and a late duke made, at his own expense, about nine hundred miles of road through it, with bridges, etc., and all without a turnpike gate.

"Above the principal windows, the motto "*Sans Peur*" is carved in raised and fanciful characters, with date, initials, etc. The interior of the building, the lobby, and stairs are faced with Caen stone. The dining-room is forty by twenty-three feet. The drawing-room windows overlook the sea, and command an extensive view. The state rooms, or "Queen's apartments," as they are called, are richly furnished

H

and ornamented.   Below is a terrace walk, a slope covered with noble trees, and parterres, winding walks, etc., the sea terminating the whole, and forming the most prominent, as it is the grandest, feature of the landscape."

The family of the Duke of Sutherland descends, as stated in a previous article, from Sir Allan Gower, Lord of Stittenham, in Yorkshire, or, as supposed by others, from William Fitz Guyer, of Stittenham, living in the year 1167.

DRAKELOWE HALL,

DERBYSHIRE has been styled by Kinder the "Amphitheatre of Renowned Persons," who further stated that "no countie in England had so many princelie habitations;" and it is no less distinguished for the numerous fine mansions it contains at the present day.

This was an ancient seat of the Gresleys, and is described in Domesday Book as belonging to Nigel de Stafford, an ancestor of the family, who held it by the service of rendering a bow with a string, a quiver of Tutesbit, a word the meaning of which appears to be now unknown, with twelve fleched arrows, and one unfeathered shaft.

Another record, of the date of 1200, describes the service to have been a bow, a quiver, and twelve arrows.

In the year 1330 Geoffrey de Gresley claimed the somewhat unsatisfactory right of having a gallows at Drakelowe, and also at Gresley.

The mansion stands on low ground, and hence, as is supposed, its name.

It is a large irregular pile.

The family of Des Vœux derives from

PRESIDENT DE BACQUENCOURT of the Parliament of Rouen, who had two sons, the second of whom,

ANTHONY VINCHON DE BACQUENCOURT, a man of great learning, left the Church of Rome for the Reformed Faith, and wrote against the Jansenists, as also on the subject of miracles, and translated and published a commentary on the book of Ecclesiastes; the last named work was considered of so much value that the University of Dublin conferred on him the degree of Honorary M.A. He took the surname of Des Vœux, and died in 1792, leaving, with a younger son and a daughter,

CHARLES DES VŒUX, Esq., of Indiville, in the Queen's County, Governor of Masulipatam, and second in the Council at Madras, who was created a Baronet the 1st. of September, 1787, and dying in 1814, was succeeded by his eldest son,

SIR CHARLES DES VŒUX, second Baronet, who married, first, Christina, daughter of

Richard Hird, Esq., of Rawdon, Yorkshire, and, secondly, Lady Caroline Paulet, daughter of the Marquis of Winchester, by the former of whom he had

SIR HENRY WILLIAM DES VŒUX, third Baronet, Lieutenant-Colonel in the army, High Sheriff of Derbyshire in 1864, who married, the 16th. of July, 1839, Lady Sophia Gresley, widow of Sir Roger Gresley, Bart., M.P., and daughter of George William Coventry, seventh Earl of Coventry, and became possessor of Drakelowe Hall.

PANSHANGER PARK,

NEAR HERTFORD, HERTFORDSHIRE.—EARL COWPER.

PANSHANGER is situated in the county of Hertford, about three miles from the county town of the same name.

The earlier residence of the family of Lord Cowper was at a short distance from the present one, and was called Coln Green. It was erected by Lord Chancellor Cowper at the commencement of the previous century. It was, however, pulled down in the year 1801 by the then Earl Cowper, and the present mansion built in its place a short distance from the original site.

It is a handsome house in the Gothic style of architecture, and stands on the north-east bank of the River Mimeram, and in the midst of a spacious park.

The grounds are described as being laid out with much taste, and a magnificent oak has been described by various local historians and tourists, and, among others, by Arthur Young, in his "Survey of the County of Herts.," who says of it:—"On the grounds of Panshanger is a most superb oak, which measures upwards of seventeen feet in circumference at five feet from the ground. It was called the GREAT OAK in 1709. It is very healthy, yet grows in a gravel surface, apparently as sterile as any soil whatever, but it undoubtedly extends its top root into soil of a very different quality. It is one of the finest oaks which I have seen, though twelve feet to the first bough."

The Lord Chancellor Cowper mentioned above was the first English lawyer who refused to receive the large payments known as "New Year's Gifts," which until his time the barristers and other attendants of the court had been accustomed to consider their due.

The family of Earl Cowper descends from

JOHN COWPER, an Alderman of the City of London, and Sheriff of the City in 1551. He was father of

SIR WILLIAM COWPER, created a Baronet March 4th., 1642, who was followed by his grandson,

SIR WILLIAM COWPER, M.P. for Hertford, whose eldest son,

SIR WILLIAM COWPER, an eminent lawyer, was made Lord Keeper of the Great Seal in 1705, and raised to the peerage the 9th. of November, 1706, as BARON COWPER of Wingham, in the county of Kent. He was followed successively by

WILLIAM COWPER, second Earl, in 1723.

GEORGE NASSAU COWPER, third Earl, in 1764.

GEORGE AUGUSTUS COWPER, fourth Earl, in 1789.

PETER LEOPOLD LOUIS FRANCIS NASSAU COWPER, fifth Earl, in 1799.

GEORGE AUGUSTUS FREDERICK COWPER, sixth Earl, in 1837.

FRANCIS THOMAS DE GREY COWPER, seventh Earl, in 1856.

AUDLEY END,

NEAR SAFFRON WALDEN, ESSEX.—LORD BRAYBROOKE.

THIS princely residence holds a distinguished place among the "County Seats" of England.

The old manor, which was vested in the crown, was bestowed by King Henry the Eighth on

SIR THOMAS AUDLEY, then Lord Chancellor of England, who was raised to the peerage in the year 1538 under the title of Baron Audley of Walden,—Walden Abbey having also been appropriated by the king at the dissolution of the monasteries, and bestowed on Sir Thomas together with the estate. His daughter and heiress,

MARGARET AUDLEY, married, first, Lord Henry Dudley, younger brother of the husband of Lady Jane Grey, and, secondly, having no children, she became the second of the three wives of Thomas Howard, fourth Duke of Norfolk.

Of the second marriage there were two sons,

    1. THOMAS, the heir.

    2. WILLIAM, ancestor of the Earls of Carlisle.

The eldest son,

THOMAS HOWARD, inherited from his mother the estate of Audley End, and was summoned to the House of Lords by Queen Elizabeth as Baron Howard of Walden. He was further elevated by King James on the 21st. of July, 1603, to the title of Earl of Suffolk, and was soon afterwards appointed Lord Chamberlain, and in performance of part of the routine of his office had to inspect the Houses of Parliament before the opening of the session, which he accordingly did in company with Lord Monteagle, to whom notice of the Gunpowder Plot had been given, and thus, on the 4th. of November, 1605, discovered the materials laid for the intended blowing-up of the assembled Lords and Commons. In the year 1618 he was appointed Lord High Treasurer of England, but being, as the father-in-law of the fallen courtier Robert Carr, Earl of Somerset, obnoxious to Buckingham, the new favourite, he was deprived of his office, and committed, together with his countess, to the Tower. It was this nobleman who erected the magnificent palace of Audley End. He died in 1626, leaving a large family, of whom the eldest son,

THEOPHILUS HOWARD, succeeded to the title and estate, and had a son and successor,

JAMES HOWARD, the third Earl, who, about the year 1668, sold the park and mansion to King Charles the Second for £50,000, of which £20,000 was left unpaid at the

Revolution, and in the year 1701 the demesne was re-conveyed to the family of Howard, the fifth Earl of Suffolk, he, on receiving it, relinquishing his claim upon the Crown for the balance of the debt. His descendant,

HENRY, tenth Earl of Suffolk, died without issue in 1733, when the Earldom devolved on his distant cousin,

HENRY BOWES HOWARD, fourth Earl of Buckingham.

The title to the estate of Audley End then became disputed, between the second Earl of Effingham, who claimed under a settlement made by the seventh Earl of Suffolk, and the heirs of the two daughters of the third Earl. The Courts of Law decided in favour of the latter, namely,

THE HONOURABLE ELIZABETH GRIFFIN, wife, first of HENRY NEVILLE (GREY,) ESQ., who assumed the last surname, and secondly, of the EARL OF PORTSMOUTH, and her sister ANNE, who married WILLIAM WHITWELL, ESQ. Of these two ladies, the former had no children, but the latter had a son, in whose favour the abeyance was terminated as

LORD HOWARD OF WALDEN. He had no children, and consequently, in consideration of his mother being sprung from the great house of Neville, he obtained for himself another barony, that of BRAYBROOKE, with a remainder to his relative Richard (Aldworth) Neville, son of Richard Aldworth, Esq., who was maternally descended from that family.

On the death of Lord Howard, in 1797, he was succeeded by the said

RICHARD NEVILLE, as second Lord Braybrooke, who was followed by

RICHARD NEVILLE, third Lord Braybrooke, father of

RICHARD CORNWALLIS NEVILLE, fourth Lord, whose successor was

CHARLES CORNWALLIS NEVILLE, fifth heir to the title.

The vast pile of Audley End is said to have cost no less than £190,000, a stupendous sum measured by the value of money in those days. It has received several subsequent alterations, but for the most part has been treated with good taste, and well preserved.

There are many valuable portraits in the house, and among them one of Lord Chamberlain Audley, by Holbein, and one of his daughter, the Duchess of Norfolk, by Lucas de Heere.

20 DE 68

The family of Lord Braybrooke derives in the male line from Richard Aldworth, Esq., of Stanlake, living in the middle of the eighteenth century.

MOUNT EDGECOMBE,

I KNOW no more lovely spot between Cornwall and the Grampians than that on which stands the noble seat which at present should be described, but in fact no description could do justice to its varied features, the scenes on every side and in every point of view being as rich and beautiful as it is possible to imagine.

Tradition states that the Duke of Medina Sidonia was so enchanted with the view of it from the sea, that never doubting of the triumphant success of the Invincible Armada, he at once determined that it should be his portion of the spoils expected from conquered England; but "the race is not always to the swift, nor the battle to the strong."

There are a number of very fine and large cork trees in the grounds near the sea, at least there were when I saw them many years ago.

This place was anciently called West Stonehouse, belonging to a family of the same name, and was conveyed by an heiress to

STEPHEN DURNFORD, ESQ., and he dying without male issue, his daughter,

JANE DURNFORD, became the wife of Sir Piers Edgecombe, K.B., a gentleman of a very ancient family in Devonshire, who derived their surname from a place of the same name in the county. He was direct ancestor of the present proprietor.

The Christian names of Piers and Richard seem to have alternated in this family for many generations, and on this "quaint old Fuller" remarks, and I have thought the same to myself in noticing the like habit or custom in the pedigrees of other families:—"The names of Pierce, or Peter, and Richard, have been (saith my author) successively varied in this family for six or seven descents. Such chequering of Christian names serves heraulds instead of stairs, whereby they ascend with assurance into the pedigrees of gentlemen; and I could wish the like alternation of font-names fashionable in other families; for where the heirs of an house are of the same name for many generations together, it occasioneth much mistake, and the most cautious and conscientious heraulds are guilty of making incestuous matches, confounding the father for the son, and so reciprocally."

This family descends from William de Edgecombe, living in the reign of Edward the Third, and who died in 1380. After him came

WILLIAM EDGCOMB.

PETER EDGECOMB.

SIR RICHARD EDGECOMB.

SIR PIERS EDGECOMBE, K.B.

SIR RICHARD EDGECOMBE, High Sheriff of Devonshire.

PETER EDGECOMBE, M.P. for the county of Cornwall in the reign of Queen Elizabeth.

SIR RICHARD EDGECOMBE.

PIERS EDGECOMBE, ESQ.

SIR RICHARD EDGECOMBE.

RICHARD EDGECOMBE, ESQ., elevated to the Peerage in 1742 as BARON EDGECOMBE.

RICHARD EDGECOMBE, second Baron.

GEORGE EDGECOMBE, third Baron, created VISCOUNT MOUNT EDGECOMBE AND VALLETORT in 1781, and EARL OF MOUNT EDGECOMBE in 1789.

RICHARD MOUNT EDGECOMBE, second Earl.

ERNEST AUGUSTUS MOUNT EDGECOMBE, third Earl, D.C.L., F.R.S., F.S.A., A.D.C. to the Queen, and Colonel of the Cornwall Militia.

WILLIAM HENRY MOUNT EDGECOMBE, fourth Earl, previously M.P. for Plymouth.

PENRYHN CASTLE,

RODERICK MOLWYNOG, Sovereign of North Wales in the eighth century, was the owner of Penryhn Castle at the early date of 720.

It was razed to the ground by Meredydd ap Owen in the year 987, who invaded the country, and slew the then remaining monarch, Cadwallan ap Jevaf.

In the time of Llewellyn it was granted, with other estates, to

YARDDUR AP TRAHAIARN, from whom, by the law of gavelkind, it descended to an heiress, who by her marriage conveyed it to the family of a descendant of Ednyfed Vychan.

GWILLYM AP GRYFFYDD possessed it in the reign of King Henry the Sixth, and was followed by his son,

WILLIAM VYCHAN AP GWILLYM, after whom came

SIR WILLIAM GRYFFYDD, in the reign of King Henry the Eighth. His grand-nephew, Piers Gryffydd, sailed in his own ship in April, 1588, and shared with Sir Francis Drake in the defeat of the Spanish Armada. He died without male issue, but a descendant of another branch of the same family, namely,

PIERS GRYFFYDD, sold the estate to his cousin,

THE RIGHT REV. DR. JOHN WILLIAMS, Lord Keeper, and Archbishop of York, who died in 1649, when this enormous property devolved to his nephew,

GRYFFYDD WILLIAMS, who in 1661 was created a Baronet, and became the father of nineteen children, of whom the eldest,

SIR ROBERT WILLIAMS, BARONET, was followed by his elder son,

SIR JOHN WILLIAMS, BARONET, who died in 1683, and was succeeded by his brother,

SIR GRYFFYDD WILLIAMS, at whose decease, also unmarried, his vast estates passed to his three sisters and co-heiresses, namely,

1. FRANCES WILLIAMS, who married Lord Edward Russell, son of the Duke of Bedford. She died without issue, and left her share of the property to her sisters.

2. ANNE WILLIAMS, married to Thomas Warburton, Esq., of Winnington, in the county of Chester.

3. GWEN WILLIAMS, married Sir Walter Yonge, Baronet, of Escott, in Devonshire.

The sole daughter and heiress of Mr. and Mrs. Warburton,

MISS WARBURTON, married Lord Penryhn, and his father, John Pennant, Esq., purchased the other moiety of the property, which went next to

GEORGE HAY DAWKINS, ESQ., cousin of Lord Penryhn, who assumed in consequence

the surname of Pennant.   His daughter married the Hon. Colonel Edward Gordon
Douglas, M.P., who also assumed the additional surname of Pennant.   She had
several children, and in favour of her family the title of Lord Penryhn was revived
in 1868.

The house is supposed to have been rebuilt by Gwillym ap Gryffydd, in the reign
of Henry the Sixth, long after its demolition by Meredydd ap Owen.

"The buildings enclose a large area or quadrangle, with gateway tower, a vast
hall, saloon, and many very elegant apartments.

"The grounds are extensive and well wooded; they command many very fine
views, receiving additional beauty from the river Ogwen, which here forms several
cascades, seen through the vistas in the plantations from the front of the house."

The family of Lord Penryhn descends from a common ancestor with that of the
Earl of Morton, namely, Sir James de Douglas, of Loudon, living about the year
1300.

WYTHAM ABBEY,

WYTHAM, or Witham Abbey, for so the name is differently or indifferently spelt, is situated about three miles from the city of Oxford, on a rising ground above the bank of the river Isis.

Here was in ancient times a nunnery, removed from its previous settlement in the neighbouring town of Abingdon, where it had been first established, but, as may without difficulty be supposed, nothing but the name of the ancient pile remains.

The more modern edifice was built in the reign of King Henry the Seventh by Sir Richard Harcourt, who became possessed of the manor of Wytham in 1480.

It seems, however, from the present form of the windows that some alterations were made in the original structure during the reign of Queen Elizabeth, or that of King James the First.

"In early days the neighbourhood became celebrated as the site of the so-called *Berkshire Tragedy*, which was booked into a ballad still preserved in the Roxburgh Collection under the name of *Wittain Miller*. The case was one unfortunately of too common occurrence, and the song which records it, though enshrined with other valueless rarities, might have been left to its proper fate without much loss to any one."

The family of Lord Abingdon derives in the male line from Robert Bertie, Lord of Bersted, near Maidstone, in Kent, living in the fifteenth century, who is stated to have been descended from the Berties, Free Barons of Bertielaw, in Prussia.

In the female line his lordship deduces his descent from the family of Norreys (afterwards Norris,) of which

JOHN NORREYS, of Bray, was ancestor of

SIR WILLIAM NORRIS, of Yattenden, in the county of Berks, one of the Knights of the body to King Edward the Fourth.

To him succeeded successively, if so one may say,

SIR EDWARD NORRIS,

SIR HENRY NORRIS,

SIR HENRY NORRIS, summoned to Parliament as Baron Norris of Rycote.

FRANCIS NORRIS, second Baron, who married Lady Bridget de Vere, daughter of Edward, Earl of Oxford, and had an only daughter and heiress,

THE HONOURABLE ELIZABETH NORRIS, who married Edward Ray, Esq., Groom of the Bedchamber to King James the First, and was mother of an only daughter and heiress,

BRIDGET WRAY, who wedded the Honourable Edward Sackville, second son of Edward, fourth Earl of Dorset, and secondly, Montagu, Earl of Lindsey, (his second wife,) and by the latter had, with other issue,

THE HONOURABLE JAMES BERTIE, who was also summoned to Parliament as Baron Norreys of Rycote, in 1675, and further raised in the peerage as Earl of Abingdon, 30th. of November, 1682.

He was succeeded by his eldest son,

MONTAGU BERTIE, second Earl of Abingdon, whose nephew,

WILLOUGHBY BERTIE, third Earl, was followed by his eldest surviving son,

WILLOUGHBY BERTIE, fourth Earl, and he by

MONTAGU BERTIE, D.C.L., High Steward of Abingdon, and Lord Lieutenant of Berkshire, who was followed by

MONTAGU BERTIE, fifth Earl, one of the co-heirs to the Barony of WILLIAMS OF THAME.

EDEN HALL,

NEAR PENRITH, CUMBERLAND.—MUSGRAVE, BARONET.

"THE martial and warlike family" of Musgrave, as it is styled by Camden, the author of the "Britannia," was originally of Musgrave, in Westmoreland, but coming into possession of Eden Hall by the marriage of Thomas de Musgrave with Joan de Stapleton, this thereupon became their seat, and has so continued till the present day.

It is a lovely spot, situated in the forest of Inglewood, and was first granted to Henry Fitzweine, and afterwards belonged to one

ROBERT TURFE, whose grandson,

ROBERT TURFE, left two daughters his co-heiresses, one of whom,

JULIAN TURFE, wedded, A.D. 1327, WILLIAM STAPLETON, and their descendants held the property for four generations, when it was carried to the family of

MUSGRAVE, as above stated.

The house is a handsome building of stone, and among other ancient reliques which it contains, is the famous old glass cup called "The Luck of Eden Hall." The sacred monogram I.H.S. shows it to have been hallowed in old times by Church use, but tradition records it to have been seized from a company of fairies who were sporting near a spring in the garden, and who, having vainly endeavoured to recover it, vanished into air singing,

> "If that glass either break or fall,
> Farewell the luck of Eden Hall."

It has not fallen or been broken yet, and is preserved with the greatest care, being only used on far-between occasions, when it is filled to the brim with wine of the rarest vintage, and whoever takes it into his hand is expected to drain it at a draught.

One of the ancestors of the present family,

SIR PHILIP MUSGRAVE, fought gallantly under the royal banner at Marston Moor, at Worcester, and in the Isle of Man, and after the Restoration had a warrant raising him to the peerage as Baron Musgrave of Hartley Castle, but the patent was never taken out. His grand-uncle, Thomas Musgrave, had a controversy with Lancelot Carleton, and the following indenture shows the ancient form and manner of proceeding to a trial of arms at single combat:—

"It is agreed between Thomas Musgrave and Lancelot Carleton, for the true trial of such controversies as are betwixt them, to have it openly tried by way of combat, before God and the face of the world, in Canonby Holme, before England and Scotland, upon Thursday in Easter week, being the 8th. day of April next ensuing, A.D. 1602, betwixt nine of the clock and one of the same day: to fight on foot; to be armed with jack and steel caps, plaite sleeves, plaite breeches, plaite socks, two swords, the blades to be one yard and half a quarter of length, two Scotch daggers or dirks at their girdles, and either of them to provide armour and weapons for themselves, according to this indenture. Two gentlemen to be appointed in the field to view both the parties, to see that they both be equal in arms and weapons, according to this indenture; and being so viewed, the gentlemen to ride to the rest of the company, and to leave them; but two boys, received by the gentlemen, to be under sixteen years of age, to hold their horses. In testimony of this our agreement, we have both set our hands to this indenture of intent: all matters shall be made so plain as there shall be no questions to stick upon that day; which indenture as a witness shall be delivered to two gentlemen; and for that it is convenient the world should be privy to every particular of the ground of the quarrel, we have agreed to set it down in this indenture betwixt us, that, knowing the quarrel, their eyes may be witness of the trial.

"The grounds of the quarrel:—

"1. Lancelot Carleton did charge Thomas Musgrave, before the Lords of Her Majesty's Privy Council, that Lancelot Carleton was told by a gentleman, one of Her Majesty's sworn servants, that Thomas Musgrave had offered to deliver Her Majesty's Castle of Bewcastle to the King of Scots; and to which the same Lancelot Carleton had a letter under the gentleman's own hand for his discharge.

"2. He charged him that, whereas Her Majesty doth yearly bestow a great fee upon him as Captain of Bewcastle, to aid and defend Her Majesty's subjects, therein Thomas Musgrave hath neglected his duty, for that Her Majesty's Castle of Bewcastle was, by him, made a den of thieves, and an harbour and receipt for murderers, felons, and all sorts of misdemeanours, etc.

"Thomas Musgrave doth deny all this charge, and saith, that he will prove that Lancelot Carleton doth falsely belie him, and will prove the same by way of combat, according to the indenture. Lancelot Carleton hath entertained the challenge, and, by God's permission, will prove it true as before; and hath set his hand to the same."

"Thomas Musgrave.
"Lancelot Carleton."

27 FE69

LOWTHER CASTLE.

LOWTHER CASTLE,

NEAR CLIFTON, WESTMORELAND.—EARL OF LONSDALE.

———

THE castle of Lowther, which gives its name to the family of Lowther, derives its own from the river Lowther, or Louder, by which it is watered.

Lowther Hall of the older date was pulled down in the year 1685, and rebuilt by John, first Viscount Lowther. It was burnt to the ground in 1720, that is to say, the two wings excepted.

It was built again in 1808, the necessary materials of stone and timber having been collected for the purpose previously by the above-mentioned first Earl Lowther.

The north front, which is surmounted by eight lofty turrets, is four hundred and twenty feet long. In the centre of it is a noble open porch large enough for the entrance of carriages.

The south front is two hundred and eighty feet long, the grand saloon being in the middle, and other magnificent apartments on either side of it. The view to the north embraces the Beacon Hill near Penrith, Saddleback, which rises three thousand and forty-eight feet above the level of the sea, and the mountains of Scotland in the distance.

The great terrace is nearly a mile in length, and overlooks a portion of the park with its forest trees of large growth and scattered herds of antlered deer.

"In Henry the Second's time the manor of Lowther would seem to have been divided into three parts, for in that reign Humphrey Machel gave a third part of the Church of Lowther to the priory of Carlisle. In 1278 one of these portions was divided between co-heiresses, married to Robert de Morville and Gilbert de Whiteby, while the other two pertained to the priory of Wotton and William de Strickland. In the year 1309 it was held of the Cliffords by the heir of John de Coupland, Henry de Haverington, Simon de Alve, and the priory of Wotton; and in 1314 the moiety of Simon de Alve was possessed by Hugh de Lowther. In 1421 Sir Robert de Lowther held the whole of this manor by the cornage of twenty shillings and fourpence."

The following is the account of the impression the beauty of the place made upon Lord Macartney, who had seen more of the world than most people:—"I wandered in *Van-shoo-quen*, or the *Paradise of Ten Thousand Trees*, for several hours, and yet was never weary of wandering, for certainly so rich, so beautiful, so sublime a prospect my eyes had never beheld. But if any place can be said in any respect to have similar features to the western part of Van-shoo-quen, which I have seen this day, it is at Lowther Hall, in Westmoreland, which, when I knew it many years ago, from the extent of prospect, the grand surrounding objects, the noble situation, the diversity of surface, and command of water, I thought might be rendered by a man of taste the finest scene in the British dominions."

The family of Lord Lonsdale descends more immediately from Sir Richard Lowther, living in the reign of Elizabeth, but its more remote ancestry is lost in the mists of antiquity, its "local habitation" being unquestionably that above indicated.

UGBROOKE,

NEAR CHUDLEIGH, DEVONSHIRE.—LORD CLIFFORD.

THE name of this seat, Ugbrooke, or Wogbrooke, is derived from that of the river by which it stands, the word *wog* in the Saxon language meaning, according to Chapple, winding, crooked, or bending.

The house, which stands on the side of an eminence, is about one mile from Chudleigh, and being in the beautiful county of Devonshire, it may well be supposed that within the circumference of seven miles of the estate there is an almost endless succession of enchanting views.—

"Collected here,
As in one point, all Nature's charms appear;
Hills strive with woods, with waters woods agree,
Of Devon's charms the grand epitome.
To those who judge by studied rules of art,
And make the whole subservient to a part,
Whose taste the neat parterre and formal line,
Or studded clumps and circling path confine,
Misshapen, rude, and rough, the draught may seem;
The great sublime was never meant for them.
O'er opening vales see hills on hills arise,
New objects vary still, and still surprise.
Through all those wilds our eyes unbounded roam
O'er half the sphere, and still confess their home;
For still no bounds their several parts control,
Rocks, hills, and plains form one united whole.
See Haldown here his russet length extends,
There Dart's high Torr in cloud-capp'd pomp ascends;
Around the horizon, broken and uneven,
Rocks frown o'er rocks, and prop the bending heaven.
Scoop'd out by Nature's hand then back they slide
In wild disorder, and the chain divide;
With bulky pride then swelling out again,
They crowd along, and break upon the plain.
The lovely plain, in pleasing contrast, now
More brightly smiles, and softens all below.
Here the majestic King with conscious pride,
Pours from his urn the tributary tide;

> Now, hid in shade, he works his silent flood
> Thro' the dark mazes of the pendant wood;
> Now murmurs on and bursting into day,
> O'er chiding pebbles rolls himself away;
> Then turns and winds his current back again,
> As loth to leave the sweet alluring plain,
> Till, sweeping through the fields with wider sway,
> He rides along and rushes to the sea.
> Here rich Pomona, too, with apples crown'd,
> Scatters her fruits and sparkling nectar round.
> See, cheerful industry walks o'er the plain,
> With all the rural graces in her train;
> On verdant slopes while Pan his flock surveys,
> And golden Ceres all her stores displays."

Thus also the plain prose of the county historian Polwhele,—"The scenery of Ugbrook is very different from that of Mamhead and Powderham. The romantic wilderness of the former may be contrasted with the comparatively tame beauties of the latter. Ugbrook hath all within itself. Powderham and Mamhead, particularly the latter, derive half their charms from distant prospect. Here the woods sweep wildly round, pursuing the course of the valley. Here the park presents to us the finest features of extensive lawn, smooth and verdant, noble eminences, and magnificent masses of shadow. Here the gigantic oaks, and other forest trees, some throwing their extravagant arms across the stream, others wreathing high their old fantastic roots, and the various windings of the brook, at one time almost hid within its rugged banks, at another whitening as it struggles amidst fragments of rocks, at another gliding over its marble bed, are points which cannot but attract admiration."

The entrance to the mansion is by a spacious hall, which opens into a dining-room thirty-six feet long by twenty-four, and on its walls are some valuable portraits by Sir Peter Lely, and a splendid painting by Titian. The library is also a room of large proportions, and is well filled with a valuable collection of ancient and modern books, and in the other rooms are a variety of articles of rarity and value.

Tradition states that this was a favourite retreat of the poet Dryden, and one of the pathways, still called Dryden's walk, commemorates the fact.

Lord Clifford derives his descent from

RICHARD FITZ PONZ, living in the reign of Henry the Second, whose son,

WALTER FITZ PONZ, married Margaret, daughter and heiress of Ralph de Todeni, with whom he acquired Clifford Castle, in Herefordshire, and hence assumed the name of Clifford.

CORSHAM COURT,

This was anciently a royal mansion, and used to be a portion of the dowry of the Queens of England. As such it was at one time possessed by Henrietta Maria, the queen of Charles the First. The name was sometimes written as it is still pronounced—Cosham, and as such it is thus described by Leland in his "Itinerary:"—

"Cosham is a good uplandish town, where the ruins of an old manor-place, and thereby a park, wont to be dower to the Queens of England. Mr. Baynton, in Queen Anne's days, pulled down, by license, a piece of this house, somewhat to help his buildings at Bromham. Old Mr. Bonhomme told me that Cosham appertained to the Earldom of Cornwall, and that Cosham was a mansion-place belonging to it, where they sometimes lay. All the men of this townlet were bond; so that upon a time one of the Earls of Cornwall hearing them secretly lament their fate, manumitted them for money, and gave them the lordship of Cosham in copyhold, to pay a chief rent."

The house was originally built by

John Thorp, Esq., in the year 1582, and was next the property of the family of Hungerford, from whom it passed to that of

Methuen.

There is here an extremely valuable collection of paintings, some of them considered the *chef-d'œuvres* of their respective masters; among others Rubens, Titian, Guido, Correggio, Paul Veronese, Michael Angelo, etc., etc.

The family of Methuen is of foreign extraction, and is stated to have derived from a German of distinction who had accompanied Queen Margaret from Hungary about the year 1070, and on whom Malcolm Canmore, King of Scotland, bestowed the Barony of Methven in Perthshire.

John Methven was Secretary of State in Scotland in the year 1440.

John Methven, of Bishop Cannings, in Wiltshire, in the reigns of King William the Third and Queen Anne, Chancellor of Ireland and Ambassador to Portugal, was father of

SIR PAUL METHUEN, K.B., a minister of these sovereigns, one of the Secretaries of State, Ambassador to Madrid, and Comptroller of the household. His cousin,

PAUL METHUEN, ESQ., M.P. for Warwick, was followed by

PAUL COBB METHUEN, ESQ., M.P. for Great Bedwin, whose son,

PAUL METHUEN, ESQ., M.P. for Wiltshire in several Parliaments, was raised to the Peerage in 1838 as Baron Methuen of Corsham, and had several children, of whom the eldest surviving son was

FREDERICK HENRY PAUL METHUEN, Lieutenant-Colonel of the Wiltshire Militia, who succeeded as second Lord Methuen.

WIMPOLE HALL,

NEAR ROYSTON, CAMBRIDGESHIRE.—EARL OF HARDWICKE.

THIS has been described as the most splendid seat in the county of Cambridge.

It is a brick mansion of spacious extent, with two wide-spreading wings, the one on the eastern side being flanked by the outbuildings, and that on the west by a large greenhouse.

The entrance to the hall is by a double flight of steps, and the principal feature of the interior is a state drawing-room, obtained by throwing several rooms into one.

Like so many of the houses of the nobility and gentry of England, the present one contains a magnificent collection of paintings, many by the old and great masters.

There is also a very fine piece of mosaic in the dining-room, representing the temple of the Sybil, and so elaborately executed that at a little distance it could not be distinguished from a painting.

The library is also a room of large size, furnished with a valuable collection of books, and a series of portraits of the most celebrated authors.

There is a private chapel within the house, the walls of which are embellished with the figures of saints, etc.

Nature has not done much for Cambridgeshire in the way of scenery, but all that art can do to improve existing materials has been done, and fine timber and sheets of water make a pleasing landscape here as elsewhere.

There is an avenue, also, two miles and a half long, of majestic trees.

The village church is situated close to the east end of the house. It was rebuilt by Lord Chancellor Hardwicke, in the year 1742, and contains some fine painted windows.

In the Chicheley Chapel, or monument room, adjoining this, are several elegant monuments.

The family of Lord Hardwicke is derived from

SIMON YORKE, of Dover, Merchant, who died in 1682. The descents since have been as follows:—His son,

PHILIP YORKE, a solicitor of respectability at Dover.

PHILIP YORKE, an eminent barrister, Solicitor-general in 1720, Attorney-general in 1724, Lord Chief Justice of England in 1733, and created BARON HARDWICKE of

Hardwicke, in the month of November of the same year. He was constituted Lord High Chancellor of England 1736, and further raised in the Peerage in 1754 to the Viscountcy of ROYSTON and Earldom of HARDWICKE. After him came his son,

PHILIP YORKE, second EARL HARDWICKE, whose nephew,

PHILIP YORKE, K.G., D.C.L., F.R.S., and F.A.S., third Earl, Lord Lieutenant of Ireland from 1801 to 1806, was followed by his nephew,

CHARLES PHILIP YORKE, F.R.S., fourth Earl of Hardwicke.

27 FE69

CASSIOBURY PARK,

NEAR WATFORD, HERTFORDSHIRE.—EARL OF ESSEX.

OFFA, King of Mercia, was the first possessor of these lands of whom we read, and they were by him bestowed on the Abbey of St. Albans. On the demolition of the monasteries by King Henry the Eighth, that monarch granted the estate to

RICHARD MORRISON, ESQ., who was one of his trusted agents. His grandson, in the reign of Charles the First,

—— MORRISON, married Mary, second daughter of Lord Campden, and having no male heir, it became the property of their heiress,

ELIZABETH MORRISON, who married Arthur, Lord Capel, of Hadham, in the county of Hertford, ancestor of the Earls of Essex.

The family mansion of Cassiobury stands in an extensive and well-wooded park, through which the river Gade flows.

It has long been celebrated for its collection of paintings, both as portraits of illustrious characters, and also as exquisite works of art. In the former of these classes may be enumerated—Algernon, Earl of Northumberland; his daughter Elizabeth, wife and widow of the first Lord Capel; Lady Anne and Lord Percy, by Vandyke; the Earl and Countess of Clarendon, by Sir Peter Lely; Sir Charles Hanbury Williams; Charles I., by Vandyke; Charles II., by Sir Peter Lely; etc. Amongst the latter may be numbered a Virgin and Child, by Carlo Maratti; a Monk's Head, by Carlo Dolce; Two Small Views, by Canaletti; a Sea Piece, by Vander Velde; a Landscape, by Gainsborough; a Landscape, by Wouvermann; etc.

The state bedroom is also noticeable for the Gobelin Tapestry in it, representing a Village Feast, copied from a painting by Teniers.

The Earls of Essex derive their descent from

JOHN CAPEL, ESQ., of Stoke Nayland, in Suffolk, father of

SIR WILLIAM CAPEL, KNIGHT, Alderman of London, and Lord Mayor in 1503. The successive descents after him have been,

SIR GILES CAPEL, next, his brother,

SIR EDWARD CAPEL, then his son,

SIR HENRY CAPEL, his son,

SIR ARTHUR CAPEL, followed by his grandson,

II. L

ARTHUR CAPEL, ESQ., created Baron Capel of Hadham.

ARTHUR CAPEL, second Baron, created VISCOUNT MALDEN and EARL OF THE COUNTY OF ESSEX in 1661.

ALGERNON CAPEL, second Earl.

WILLIAM CAPEL, third Earl.

WILLIAM ANNE CAPEL, fourth Earl.

GEORGE CAPEL, fifth Earl.

ARTHUR ALGERNON CAPEL, sixth Earl.

BADMINTON HOUSE,

NEAR TETBURY, GLOUCESTERSHIRE.—DUKE OF BEAUFORT.

THE first possessor of Badminton on record was one

EDRICK, who held it in the reign of King Edward the Confessor. Next

ERNULF DE ESDING owned it in the time of the Conqueror, and afterwards it was held for several centuries by the family of

BOTELER, until

NICHOLAS BOTELER, in the year 1608, sold the estate to

THE HONOURABLE SIR THOMAS SOMERSET, K.B., third son of Edward, fourth Earl of Worcester, who in the year 1626 was created Viscount Somerset of Cashel, in the county of Tipperary, in Ireland. He left an only daughter and heiress,

ELIZABETH SOMERSET, who dying unmarried, bequeathed the Castle to

HENRY, LORD HERBERT, afterwards created Duke of Beaufort.

The park is very extensive, being nearly ten miles in circumference.

The house within is splendidly decorated.

In the great dining-room is a large quantity of valuable carving in wood by Grinling Gibbons.

The picture gallery contains a fine series of family portraits. The most remarkable of the others is a satirical painting by Salvator Rosa, for which he was expelled from Rome. There also may be found the head of Guido, by himself; one of Cardinal Alberoni, by Trevisani; of Erasmus and Sir Thomas More, by Holbein; and of Cornelius Jansen, by himself. Also several excellent landscapes by Italian masters, The Holy family, by Raphael, and other much-admired pictures by Guido and Carlo Dolce.

Badminton was visited in the year 1702 by Queen Anne and her Consort, Prince George of Denmark.

The family of the Duke of Beaufort derives from Charles Somerset, an illegitimate son of Henry, Duke of Somerset, K.G., himself descended from an illegitimate son of John of Gaunt, Duke of Lancaster, son of King Edward the Fourth. He married Elizabeth, only daughter and heiress of William Herbert, Earl of Huntingdon, Lord Herbert of Ragland, Chepstow, and Gower, and was summoned to Parliament as such in the first year of Henry the Eighth. He was created EARL OF WORCESTER for the distinguished part he had in the taking of Tournay and Terouenne. He was father of

HENRY SOMERSET, second Earl, whose son,

WILLIAM SOMERSET, K.G., third Earl, was followed by his son,

EDWARD SOMERSET, fourth Earl, created VISCOUNT SOMERSET of Cashel, in the county of Tipperary. His eldest surviving son was

HENRY SOMERSET, fifth Earl, advanced to the dignity of the MARQUIS OF WORCESTER, November 2nd., 1642. His eldest son was

EDWARD SOMERSET, second Marquis. He published a work in which the power and application of the steam engine are distinctly described. His son,

HENRY SOMERSET, third Marquis, was created DUKE OF BEAUFORT, December 2nd., 1682. His grandson succeeded as

HENRY SOMERSET, second Duke, and he by his elder son,

HENRY SOMERSET, third Duke. He by his brother,

CHARLES NOEL SOMERSET, fourth Duke. He by

HENRY SOMERSET, fifth Duke, followed by

HENRY CHARLES SOMERSET, sixth Duke.

HENRY SOMERSET, K.G., seventh Duke.

CHARLES FITZROY SOMERSET, P.C., eighth Duke.

DANBURY PALACE,

IF this ancient seat had from the first been a seat of the Bishop of Rochester, one could not wonder at the number of its numerous proprietors, inasmuch as it is but very seldom that in the course of ecclesiastical affairs, a bishop, though he may live to an old age, holds the see for a lengthened period, and we do not therefore think it strange to read, when there is a new bishop appointed to this or that diocese, that he is the eightieth or ninetieth who has held that post.

But in truth it is only very recently that this place has been the residence of the Bishops of Rochester. It has, however, even before it became such, changed hands a remarkable number of times, as will appear from the following brief history of its successive proprietors:—

In the reign of Edward the Confessor it was held by one

ARLING, a Saxon, and next, about the time of the compilation of "Domesday Book," namely, in the reign of William the Conqueror, it was the property of

GEFFERY DE MANDEVILLE. Soon afterwards the greater part of it came to the family of

DE SANTO CLARO, or ST. CLARE, and the estate is still called St. Clare's Manor. From them it passed successively to the families of

DE VERE, EARLS OF OXFORD.

DE GREY, of Wilton.

SIR GERARD BRAYBROOKE.

LORD DARCY, and then fell to the Crown.

It was next granted by King Edward the Sixth, to

WILLIAM PARR, Mayor of Nottingham, who alienated it to

SIR WALTER MILDMAY, KNIGHT, founder of Emmanuel College, Cambridge, who died in 1559, and by whom the Mansion House of Danbury Palace was erected. After him,

SIR MATTHEW MILDMAY was succeeded by his second son,

HUMPHREY MILDMAY, High Sheriff of Essex, in the eleventh year of Charles the First's reign, and was followed by

JOHN MILDMAY, ESQ., whose daughter,

MARY MILDMAY, married William Fytche, Esq., of Woodham Walter. It afterwards became the seat of

JOHN ROUND, ESQ., M.P. for Maldon in 1845.

It appears also to have been formerly held by the family of

RICH, and also by that of

WESTON.

Finally, it was purchased by the Ecclesiastical Commissioners, with the proceeds of the sales of the Palaces of Bromley and Rochester, as a residence for the Bishops of Rochester.

It was anciently a Peculiar of the Archbishop of Canterbury, and subject to the special jurisdiction of the Dean of Bocking.

It stands on one of the highest eminences in the county, and is situated about six miles from Chelmsford, four from Maldon, and thirty-three from London.

CLUMBER PARK,*

NEAR OLLERTON, NOTTINGHAMSHIRE.—DUKE OF NEWCASTLE.

THIS princely seat of the Duke of Newcastle is one of the three "Dukeries." The others being, or rather having been, Welbeck Abbey, the seat of the Duke of Portland, and Worksop Manor, the seat of the Duke of Norfolk, but the last named was purchased by the then Duke of Newcastle some years since, and the mansion pulled down. It was a noble mansion when last I saw it.

The principal rooms in this great house are the state dining-room, sixty feet long, thirty-four feet wide, and thirty feet high: it can accommodate one hundred and fifty guests at dinner, with room to spare. The entrance-hall is very lofty, and the roof supported by columns.

The library of books is stated to be a most valuable collection.

The park is about thirteen miles in circumference. Clumber is named in Domesday Book as having within it before the Conquest two manors of Roger de Buisli, Adelwool and Ulchill. But to my view the great ornament of Clumber, as of every other country house where there is such, is the fine sheet of water in front of it, on which there is, at least there was when I visited it many years ago, a good-sized frigate, fitted up and rigged in the most perfect manner, not a rope or block wanting or out of place, the handiwork of some old sailor, who had left the perils of the sea to wield his crutch on land, and tell how battles had been fought and won.

The state drawing-room is forty-eight feet long by thirty-three feet wide.

The library is of similar dimensions, and last, but not least, so is the kitchen.

There is also a private chapel, four of the windows in which cost £800 each.

Here are, as may well be supposed, pictures and paintings "rich and rare." One room contains seven valued at £25,000.

Among these and others are, as to the old masters, works by Guido, Rubens, Michael Angelo, Correggio, Rembrandt, Salvator Rosa, Domenechino, Battisti Franco, Castiglione, Albert Durer, Vandyke, Teniers, Poussin, Vander-Meuden, Van Oorst, and Snyders.

As to the modern painters, Gainsborough and Sir Joshua Reynolds may be mentioned as having their niches.

* See View on the Title.

Not more than a century ago, in fact within that time, this cultivated park and estate is described as having been "a black heath full of rabbits, having a narrow river running through it."

———

The Duke of Newcastle descends from John de Clinton, of Amington, in Warwickshire, living in the year 1300. He was summoned to Parliament as Baron Clinton of Maxtock, in the county of Warwick, in 1299, February 6th. The descents afterwards were as follows:—

SIR JOHN DE CLINTON, summoned to Parliament four times as a Baron in the reign of Edward the Third.

SIR JOHN CLINTON.

SIR JOHN CLINTON, shared in the triumphs of Edward the Third and the Black Prince, and was also summoned to Parliament.

WILLIAM CLINTON, fourth LORD CLINTON.

JOHN CLINTON, fifth Lord.

JOHN CLINTON, sixth Lord.

JOHN CLINTON, seventh Lord.

THOMAS CLINTON, eighth Lord.

EDWARD CLINTON, ninth Lord, created Earl of Lincoln in 1572.

HENRY CLINTON, K.B., second Earl of Lincoln.

THOMAS CLINTON, third Earl.

THEOPHILUS CLINTON, K.B., fourth Earl.

EDWARD CLINTON, fifth Earl, followed by his cousin,

SIR FRANCIS FIENNES CLINTON, sixth Earl.

HENRY CLINTON, K.G., seventh Earl.

GEORGE CLINTON, eighth Earl, followed by his brother,

HENRY CLINTON, K.G., ninth Earl, who inherited the Dukedom of Newcastle on the death of his Countess's uncle, Thomas Pelham Holles, who had been so created in 1756, with special remainder to him.

THOMAS CLINTON, third Duke of Newcastle, and tenth Earl of Lincoln.

HENRY PELHAM CLINTON, K.G., D.C.L., fourth Duke.

HENRY PELHAM CLINTON, K.G., fifth Duke.

HENRY PELHAM ALEXANDER CLINTON, sixth Duke.

27 FE69

B. FAWCETT, ENGRAVER AND PRINTER, DRIFFIELD.

Lightning Source UK Ltd.
Milton Keynes UK
UKHW030651310321
381306UK00006B/459